Cured!

Other Titles by Dick B.

Anne Smith's Journal, 1933-1939: A.A.'s Principles of Success

By the Power of God:
    A Guide to Early A.A. Groups & Forming Similar Groups Today

Courage to Change:
    The Christian Roots of the Twelve-Step Movement (with Bill Pittman)

Dr. Bob and His Library: A Major A.A. Spiritual Source

God and Alcoholism:
    Our Growing Opportunity in the 21st Century

Good Morning!:
    Quiet Time, Morning Watch, Meditation, and Early A.A.

Hope!: The Story of Geraldine D., Alina Lodge & Recovery

Making Known the Biblical History and Roots of Alcoholics Anonymous:
    An Eleven-Year Research, Writing, Publishing, and Fact Dissemination Project

New Light on Alcoholism: God, Sam Shoemaker, and A.A.

The Akron Genesis of Alcoholics Anonymous

The Books Early AAs Read for Spiritual Growth

The Golden Text of A.A.:
    God, the Pioneers, and Real Spirituality

The Good Book and The Big Book: A.A.'s Roots in the Bible

The Oxford Group & Alcoholics Anonymous:
    A Design for Living That Works

That Amazing Grace:
    The Role of Clarence and Grace S. in Alcoholics Anonymous

Turning Point:
    A History of Early A.A.'s Spiritual Roots and Successes

Utilizing Early A.A.'s Spiritual Roots for Recovery Today

Why Early A.A. Succeeded
    The Good Book in Alcoholics Anonymous Yesterday and Today
    (A Bible Study Primer for AAs and other 12-Steppers)

Cured!
Proven Help for Alcoholics and Addicts

"Henrietta [wife of A.A. Number Three, Bill Dotson], the Lord has been so wonderful to me, curing me of this terrible disease, that I just want to keep talking about it and telling people"

        Bill Wilson (Bill W.), Co-founder of A.A.
            Alcoholics Anonymous, 4th ed., 2001, p. 191

Dick B.

Paradise Research Publications, Inc.
Kihei, Maui, Hawaii

Paradise Research Publications, Inc., P.O. Box 837, Kihei, HI 96753-0837

© 2003 by Anonymous
All rights reserved. Published 2003
Printed in the United States of America

This Paradise Research Publications Edition is published by arrangement with Good Book Publishing Company, P.O. Box 837, Kihei, Maui, HI 96753-0837

The publication of this volume does not imply affiliation with nor approval or endorsement from Alcoholics Anonymous World Services, Inc. The views expressed herein are solely those of the author. A.A. is a program of recovery from alcoholism—use of the Twelve Steps in connection with programs and activities which are patterned after A.A., but which address other problems, does not imply otherwise.

Note: Scriptures quoted in this book are from the Authorized (King James) Version of the Bible, which is identified by the letters "KJV" when necessary for clarity, unless otherwise noted.

ISBN: 1-885803-35-4

Contents

    Foreword ix
    Preface xi

1   The Earliest A.A. Days 1

    Christian Fellowship and Cure in A.A.'s Very First Group .. 1
    Specific Elements of A.A.'s Pioneer Ideas and Program 5
    The Pioneers Could and Did Help Other Drunks to Cure
        by the Power of God 9
    The Term "Cure" in Early A.A. 14
    There Were Many Specific Cures of Alcoholics
        before A.A. Began 18
    "Once an Alcoholic, Always an Alcoholic"? 18

2   Let's Use Simple Words That People Understand 19

    We Will Understand "Cure" Best When We Say "Cure" ... 19
    "Cure" Means Cure! 20
    The A.A. Pioneers Were Cured of Alcoholism 23
    Now, Just What Was This "Alcoholism"
        of Which They Had Been Cured? 28
    What, Then, Is the Cure? 31
    I Am Not Mis-applying the Word "Cure"—Just Pointing
        to the Power of God 32

3   Newcomer Netting 35

    A Life and Death Matter, As A.A. Sees It 35
    The Author's Experience, Victory, and Outreach 36
    The Victory 45
    What Does This Newcomer Stuff Mean to You? 46

4 What History Can Teach You in, and about, A.A. Itself ... 49

The "Spins" You Need to Ignore 49
History and the Big Book, A.A.'s Basic Text 50
History and the Twelve Steps 53
An Historical View: Twelve Steps and Their Main Roots .. 54
Shall You Cram *Your* Bible into Today's A.A.? 62
How Do You Help the Unbeliever? 64
How Can You Help a Believer in, or into, A.A.? 67
Do You Alter the Text and Steps to Suit Your Beliefs? 71
How a Believer Might *View* the Steps, and *Not Edit* Them . 72
Just How, Then, Can You Help a Believer 78

5 Offering More Than Abstinence 81

6 Facing "Reality" with "Divine Help" 89

"Reality" 89
Tossing out the "Nonsense gods" of Recovery 90
Alcoholics May Be Sick, but They Are Not Stupid 92
The Emphasis Needs to Be on Changing Their Lives 93

7 Talking Plainly about the Creator 95

"Finding" God 95
Talking about Almighty God 96
The Basic Text Is the Bible. "Back to Basics" Means
   Back to the Bible 97

8 There Is More to Cure Than Abstinence 101

Casting out the Misery 101
Release from *Your* Prisons 105
And Much, Much More in the Good Book 108
Toss out the Blame; Change Yourself; and
   Walk in God's Ways 109
Practical Means of Avoiding Self-destruction 111
Some Real Basics 113

Contents   vii

9   My Own Table of Tips 119

    What Has Worked Best 119
    Shooting for Long Term Goals 126

10 Cured and Victorious! Putting the Pieces Together 129

    Yes! The Alcoholic Can Be Cured 129
    Once a Leper, Always a Leper? 129
    Far More Than Cure Awaits God's Kids 132
    This Bible Stuff Need Not Drive Anyone up a Tree 134
    It Is about Victory 135
    It Is about God's Love 136

    Bibliography 137
    Index 155

Foreword

It is with great pleasure that I write this Foreword to Dick B.'s latest book. What this book lays out, in clearly researched and documented detail, is the miracle of the God-granted cure of the compulsive use of addictive substances and behaviors—a cure that has been experienced and lived out again and again—for over 60 years since the beginnings of Alcoholics Anonymous—in the lives of hundreds of thousands of alcoholics and addicts.

Once again, Dick has done his homework thoroughly, and we are the recipients of his years of research. As I read and studied this book, and continue to see the immensity and devastation that alcoholism and addiction inflict in so many lives, I was reminded of the words of William D. Silkworth, M.D.:

> Faced with this problem, if a doctor is honest with himself, he must sometimes feel his own inadequacy. Although he gives all that is in him, it often is not enough. . . . we physicians must admit we have made little impression upon the problem as a whole [*Alcoholics Anonymous*, 3rd edition, pp. xxiii].

I agree with Dr. Silkworth. I, as a physician, realize that 21st Century medicine offers what is often inadequate help and hope to those in alcoholism and addiction. As with Dr. Bob, I as a Christian, have the privilege of pointing an alcoholic and addict toward the only One Who can effect a true cure—Jesus Christ. Dick B. shows that this is exactly what the early AA's did, and with amazing success.

I continue to stand in awe of God Who can take a person "from a trembling, despairing, nervous wreck" to "emerge a man (or woman) brimming over with self-reliance and contentment" (Alcoholics Anonymous, 3rd edition, pp. xxv).

The beginnings of AA were a miraculous work of God. This is so clearly documented again and again in the writings of AA from its earliest days, such as the words of Bill Wilson, ". . . [T]he Lord has been so wonderful to me, curing me of this terrible disease. . . ." (Alcoholics Anonymous, 4th edition, p. 191)

The biblical foundation of AA is without dispute, as seen in the early literature, current Conference approved literature, and in all of Dick's books. This biblical foundation continues to be a reminder that we are all, whether we admit it consciously or not, completely reliant on The God Who has perfectly, lovingly, and tenderly revealed Himself in His Word, the Bible.

I encourage you to read and study this book; do your own homework and study to see "whether those things were so" (Acts 17:11). Thank you, Dick, for one of the most remarkable books I have ever read, one which has reminded me of the miracles that occur daily in my life and in the lives of so many around me.

Robert P. Turner, M.D.
Medical Director, MUSC Clinical Neurophysiology Laboratory
Departments of Neurology, Pediatrics, and Neurological Surgery
Medical University of South Carolina
Charleston, South Carolina

Preface

This latest of my titles on the history of early Alcoholics Anonymous cuts to the heart of my whole endeavor. This title asks quite simply, "Are we forever sick?" Or can we be healed, once and for all, by the Creator of the heavens and the earth?

This title addresses the presently-held A.A. conviction: "Once an alcoholic, always an alcoholic." It responds with an answer that will ruffle some uninformed feathers. It declares emphatically, "Never!" Never, from God's standpoint, are you incurably sick. If you were a cancer patient, would you want to hear "Once a cancer patient, always a cancer patient?" Or, as to AIDS, "Once an AIDS patient, always an AIDS patient?" Or, as to leprosy, "Once a leper, always a leper?"

You'd only want to hear such death sentences if no doctor, no clergyman, and no human power could help you at all. And, even then, only if God Almighty could not heal you. But early AAs quite clearly believed that "God ought to be able to do anything" (*e.g. Alcoholics Anonymous*, 4th ed., p. 158). The Bible puts it as an absolute: ". . . [W]ith God nothing shall be impossible" (Luke 1:37). Ephesians 3:20 declares as to God's great power: "Now unto him that is able to do exceeding abundantly above all that we ask or think, according to the power that worketh in us."

Pioneer AAs heard and read these declarations from the Good Book. And they had a choice: They could choose to continue destroying themselves; or they could choose to rely on the power of the Creator, our God.

Early AAs and their doctors had previously looked on alcoholics as the epitome of the "impossible"—medically incurable, with a seemingly hopeless condition of mind and body, "doomed," and 100% hopeless apart from divine help (See *Alcoholics Anonymous*, 4th ed., pp. xiii, xxx, 17, 43; *DR. BOB and the Good Oldtimers*, pp. 130-31).

Beginning in 1935, they opted for divine help. They put their lives in God's hands. They looked to the Creator for healing. And they were cured!

This is the story of a proven cure for alcoholics and addictions—a cure that cannot and does not fail when one becomes a child of God, and believes what God offers in the way of forgiveness, healing, and deliverance. It is also the story of what I have done within the fellowship of Alcoholics Anonymous that has proved that any alcoholic—any alcoholic at all—can be cured if he or she abstains from booze; turns to God as a Father for help; maintains fellowship with God, His Son and other like-minded believers; and witnesses to others what God can do for His kids.

This book also highlights the freedom of any alcoholic—any alcoholic at all—any time, to return to his own vomit or to wallowing in the mire (2 Peter 2:20-22). Sinful thoughts, sinful words, and sinful deeds are just as much the tempters today as they were when early AAs gave heed to the verses in James 1:13-26. God does not tempt us. But our own bad habits, bad thinking, bad words, bad deeds, bad companions, and bad environments can and do. The price of temptation may not always be drinking or death; but it certainly precludes the abundant life God's son came to make available to believers (John 10:10).

God's ways are not man's ways. God's ways are clearly defined in the Good Book. Adherence to God's ways is what the A.A. pioneers were aiming for. And you can find their proclamations in any honest report on what Dr. Bob, his Akron pioneers, and their families said and did. First, they ended their drunkenness once and for all. Then they asked God for help. Then they were cured. They were changed. They maintained daily fellowship with God. And they carried that message to others. And that is the message of this book.

1
The Earliest A.A. Days

Christian Fellowship and Cure in A.A.'s Very First Group

Truly Astonishing Miracles

By 1990, little, if anything significant, had been written about the specifics of the earliest A.A. days—the days of A.A.'s actual founding in Akron, Ohio. Little, that is, about the absolute necessity for relying on the Creator, our God; the nature and conduct of Akron's Christian Fellowship; and the Pioneer program's cure for "seemingly hopeless," "medically incurable, "real alcoholics," who "really tried." Today I still hear comments that all the pioneers died drunk; but the names of those pioneers are well known, can be found in several rosters, and debunk the myth of alleged early failures ending in drunken deaths..

Some might think A.A. is really not about, or no longer about, a mere "hard core of very grim, last-gasp cases [that] had by then [late 1937] been sober a couple of years," as Bill Wilson put it. These consisted of "upwards of 40 alcoholics . . . staying bone dry," said Bill. Some *forty* A.A. pioneers, of whom at least twenty had, for two years after A.A.'s founding in 1935, remained "bone dry"—with more than forty in the bunch having stayed dry and having "recovered"as the result of the program. This, after their having suffered countless years as very sick people (*DR. BOB and the Good Oldtimers.* NY: Alcoholics Anonymous World Services, 1980, p. 123; *Pass It On, id.*, 1984, pp. 178-79; *Alcoholics Anonymous Comes of Age, id.*, p. 76). And the success record of these forty alcoholics astonished other alcoholics, physicians, and clergy alike. It astonished them in the 1930's; and it should astonish us all today.

By late fall of 1937, seventy-five percent of the pioneer AAs had been fully cured; and twenty-five percent had shown "improvement." Nothing like this success rate had previously been seen in the inebriate wards, insane asylums, jails, missions, and hospitals that had been the habitat of the sick.

Lately I have written much about the early A.A. program and its victories. This because skilled historians have seemingly been ignoring, minimizing, or mis-characterizing the pioneer successes. A.A.'s own publications have focused on the writings of, and the Twelve Step program fostered by, A.A. co-founder Bill Wilson. Other observers—perhaps because of their religious views; their atheist or agnostic preferences; their enthusiasm for "universalizing" the fellowship; or their willingness to compromise in the interest of promoting growth—have given every appearance of wanting to just plain forget the "God-centered" miracles of Akron. Such people have lauded Bill's Big Book; "sanctified" his Twelve Steps; and focused on historical events that occurred in A.A.'s most miserable years—the 1940's. Some or all of the same people, perhaps for similar reasons, have then propagated "recovery"ideas, theologies, and practices that bear little resemblance to the original A.A. program.

The *pioneer* program—the "old school" A.A. program—was developed by Bill Wilson *and* Dr. Bob Smith (of Akron) primarily during the summer of 1935. Then it was tested, primarily in Akron, over the next two years. By late 1937, the proven results of Akron's hands-on program prompted Wilson, Smith, and Smith's wife to count noses. And the three joined in prayers of thanks that God Almighty had shown them how to pass their miracle on to others [See Dick B. *The Akron Genesis of Alcoholics Anonymous*, 2d ed. (Kihei, HI: Paradise Research Publications, 1998), pp. 224-25; *RHS*, Memorial Issue of *The Grapevine*, issued in January, 1951, on the occasion of Dr. Bob's death (NY: The A.A. Grapevine, Inc., 1951), p. 8; Robert Thomsen, *Bill W*. (New York: Harper & Row, 1975), pp. 266-67; *Pass It On* (NY: Alcoholics Anonymous World Services, Inc., 1984), pp. 177-79].

Dr Bob's and A.A.'s Own Comments on the Earliest Program

Let's look right now, and once again, at what A.A.'s own literature and A.A.'s co-founder Dr. Bob did have to say about that earliest program, as Bill and Bob developed it between 1935 and late 1937:

> [Dr. Bob stated:] We had both been associated with the Oxford Group, Bill in New York, for five months, and I in Akron, for two and a half years. Bill had acquired their idea of service. I had not, but I had done an immense amount of reading they had recommended. I had refreshed my memory of the Good Book, and I had had excellent training in that as a youngster. . . . [*The Co-Founders of Alcoholics Anonymous: Biographical sketches Their last major talks* (New York: Alcoholics Anonymous World Services, Inc., 1972, 1975), pp. 11-12]

> [Dr. Bob also said:] I am somewhat allergic to work, but I felt that I should continue to increase my familiarity with the Good Book and should also read a good deal of standard literature. So I did cultivate the habit of reading. . . . [*The Co-Founders, supra*, p. 13]

> [Dr. Bob added:] At that point, our stories didn't amount to anything to speak of. When we started in on Bill D., we had no Twelve Steps, either; we had no Traditions. But we were convinced that the answer to our problems was in the Good Book. To some of us older ones, the parts that we found absolutely essential were the Sermon on the Mount, the thirteenth chapter of First Corinthians, and the Book of James. We used to have daily meetings at a friend's house [the home of T. Henry Williams in Akron]. . . . [*The Co-Founders, supra*, p. 13]

> [Dr. Bob concluded:] It wasn't until 1938 that the teachings and efforts and studies that had been going on were crystalized in the form of the Twelve Steps. I didn't write the Twelve Steps. I had nothing to do with the writing of them. . . . Bill came to live at our house and stayed for about three months. There was hardly a night that we didn't sit up until two or three o'clock, talking. It would be hard for me to conceive that, during these nightly discussions around our kitchen table, nothing was said that influenced the writing of the Twelve Steps. *We already had the basic ideas*, though not in terse and tangible form. *We got them, as I said, as a result of our study of the Good Book.* We must

> have had them. Since then, *we have learned from experience that they were very important in maintaining sobriety* [*The Co-Founders, supra*, p. 14; emphasis added]

A.A.'s *DR. BOB and the Good Oldtimers* (NY: Alcoholics Anonymous World Services, Inc., 1980) summed up as to the Pioneers, their resources, and their efforts as follows:

> They had the Bible, and they had the precepts of the Oxford group. They also had their own instincts. They were working, or working out, the A.A. program. . . . [p. 96]

No Text Book and No Steps

Again! They had no Big Book or basic text. They had no Steps. None at all. No Twelve Steps; no "Six Steps;" and no "Four Steps." They had no Traditions. Their Oxford Group helpers had no Steps. None at all. No Twelve Steps; no "six steps;" no "four steps." No Traditions.

An Akron, Ohio, A.A. pamphlet of the 1940's—published by the Friday Forum Luncheon Club of the Akron A.A. Groups—summarized the following from a "lead" [talk, or speech] by Dr. Bob in Youngstown, Ohio:

> Members of Alcoholics Anonymous begin the day with a prayer for strength and a short period of Bible reading. They find the basic messages they need in the Sermon on the Mount, in Corinthians and the Book of James. [Dick B., *The Good Book and The Big Book: A.A.'s Roots in the Bible.* 3rd ed. (Kihei, HI: Paradise Research Publications, Inc., 1998), p. 21]

The Bible and Their Christian Fellowship

The A.A. Pioneers simply had the Bible that they studied. And they had some Oxford Group ideas. This was during the period the Oxford Group called itself "A First Century Christian Fellowship." The early AAs also were building on their experiences as drunks. Frank Amos (the man who investigated their program for John D. Rockefeller, Jr.) referred to these men as the "self-styled Alcoholic Group of Akron, Ohio."

Later, Amos reported that "in many respects, their meetings have taken on the form of the meetings described in the Gospels [sic] of the early Christians during the first century" (*DR. BOB and the Good Oldtimers, supra,* pp. 135-36). Rockefeller's other cohorts also remarked specifically on A.A.'s resemblance to First Century Christianity (Dick B., *The Good Book and The Big Book, supra,* p. 44).

When asked what the Akron alcoholic "club" was about, Dr. Bob replied that it was "A Christian fellowship" (*DR. BOB and the Good Oldtimers, supra,* p. 118). His daughter (Sue Smith Windows) told me in an interview in June, 1991, that Dr. Bob described every King School Group meeting (of A.A.) as a "Christian Fellowship." And this King School Group did not (with that name of "King School") even start meeting at King School in Akron until after the Big Book had been published in the Spring of 1939.

Specific Elements of A.A.'s Pioneer Ideas and Program

Dr. Bob's Early Youth Produced Several of Akron A.A.'s Christian Roots and Practices

There is no need to repeat here our writings on Dr. Bob's Bible study, prayer, fellowship practices, and Christian training as a youngster, in the North Congregational Church of St. Johnsbury, Vermont, where his parents were pillars of that church. Nor on the Christian elements that came from his involvement in the huge Christian Endeavor movement of that very time. [See Appendix One of Dick B., *Dr. Bob and His Library: A Major A.A. Spiritual Source*, 3rd ed. (Kihei, HI: Paradise Research Publications, 1998), pp. 111-19. See also our discussion of the Christian Endeavor principles in Dick B., *The Books Early AAs Read for Spiritual Growth*, 7th ed. (Kihei, HI: Paradise Research Publications, 1998), pp. 13-17.]

However, my materials document that the following—(1) "Confession of Christ," (2) prayer, (3) Bible study, (4) quiet time, (5) seeking God's guidance, (6) reading of Christian literature, (7) Christian Fellowship, (8) church participation, and (9) witnessing—were very much a part of Dr. Bob's religious life and training as a young person. Furthermore, those principles and practices bear much resemblance to the "Christian Fellowship," "old fashioned prayer meetings," "surrenders to Christ," and widespread reading of Christian literature that so uniquely characterized the Akron program from its inception in 1935 to at least 1938, when the writing of the Big Book was begun by Bill Wilson in New York.

Anne Ripley Smith, Dr. Bob's Wife, Also Provided Extremely Important Input

Seemingly, I have been alone among several historians, including Bill Wilson himself, when it comes to reporting on Anne Ripley Smith, the wife of A.A. co-founder Dr. Bob. I have many times described and emphasized the role that Dr. Bob's wife played in the development and success of the early A.A. program.

From 1933 to 1939, Anne assembled and wrote in her journal the principles and practices A.A. pioneers studied in the Bible, the Oxford Group, the Christian literature of the day, and put into practice with their families. In the summer of 1935, she daily read from the Bible to Dr. Bob and Bill while they were working up the original program. She shared each morning at a Quiet Time she conducted at the Smith home where A.A. was born—reading from the Bible, leading prayers, seeking guidance, and encouraging discussion of matters in her journal. She advocated daily Bible study, daily Quiet Time with prayer and listening. She recommended specific reading from the Bible, from Christian literature, from devotionals, and from Oxford Group and Shoemaker books. Her writings are filled with practical discussions of every biblical and Oxford Group principle that impacted on A.A.

For her unique services, Anne was characterized by Bill Wilson and many others as the "Mother of A.A." and a "founder" of A.A., as well as nurse, evangelist, counselor, teacher, and ever-present attender of meetings of the early group. She was regarded as unusually adept in her work with newcomers and A.A. families.

To know and study the almost forgotten contents of Anne Smith's journal is an absolute essential to knowledge of early A.A. and the real ingredients of its program. [See Dick B., *Anne Smith's Journal 1933-1939: A.A.'s Principles of Success*, 3rd ed. (Kihei, HI: Paradise Research Publications, 1998).]

The Contents of the Frank Amos Reports of 1938 to John D. Rockefeller, Jr., Spell out Most of the Specifics of the Real Pioneer "Program" of Recovery

Again. No need to repeat in this title our lengthy discussion of A.A. trustee-to-be Frank Amos's investigation of, and findings about, the real, early A.A. program. The Frank Amos investigation was thorough. It was conducted in Akron which was the crucible of the new God-centered recovery experiment. It was prompted by Bill Wilson's own approaches to Rockefeller in New York for funds. It was, and was intended to be, independent and unbiased. It was concise. It had much to do with the establishment of A.A.'s Alcoholic Foundation, precursor of A.A.'s General Service Board. And it resulted in Amos himself's becoming a non-alcoholic trustee for A.A. It is therefore authoritative, from A.A.'s own standpoint.

I have seen; I own; and I have studied authorized copies of the originals. And fortunately most of the material can be found quoted in *DR. BOB and the Good Oldtimers* (New York: Alcoholics Anonymous World Services, Inc., 1980), pp. 122-36. An extensive discussion of the Amos Reports can be found in Dick B., *God and Alcoholism: Our Growing Opportunity in the 21st Century* (Kihei, HI: Paradise Research Publications, 2002), pp. 2-12.

The Amos reports themselves, and my own extensive discussion of them, make clear the simplicity, uniqueness, and effectiveness of A.A.'s Pioneer program. I like to call that program "Old School A.A." Its essentials were: (1) Admission of alcoholism, incurable from a medical viewpoint, coupled with the willingness to stop drinking *forever*. (2) Hospitalization or medical attention at the earliest moment—in almost every case. (3) Belief in the Creator. (4) Establishment of a relationship with Him through acceptance of Jesus Christ as Lord and Saviour. (5) Obedience to God's will. (6) Removal from the alcoholic's life of the sins which were contrary to God's will and frequently accompany alcoholism. (7) Participation in Morning Quiet Time and devotions, with Bible study, prayer, and reading of Christian literature. (8) Consistently helping other alcoholics get straightened out. (9) Maintaining frequent social and religious comradeship with other ex-alcoholic believers. (10) Weekly attendance at some religious service. (11) Family participation.

And I hasten to say that *some* of the foregoing essentials are not even specifically pointed out in the Amos report; but they are documented aspects of what the Pioneers regularly did. Examples are: (a) hospitalization—which Amos does not cover; (b) belief in God and in the necessity for a new birth—which Amos merely implies in his discussion of Christian techniques and of A.A.'s then resemblance to First Century Christianity; (c) obedience to God's commandments—again a requirement implicit in Amos's emphasis on Christianity and sin, (d) family participation—which finds mention in almost every account of early Akron A.A.

Learning and understanding the foregoing eleven elements of the Akron program of the 1930's will make quite obvious to you the differences and variations between early A.A. and the elements of the A.A. program, meetings, and groups today. This knowledge will provide you with a unique view of Akron fellowship practices—practices that were mostly devoid of Oxford Group emphasis, devoid of meeting emphasis, and dedicated to reliance on the Creator. As to all of which, Dr. Bob proclaimed: "Your Heavenly Father will never let you down!" (Big Book, 4th ed., p. 181).

Note that Dr. Bob did not declare that going to meetings, studying the basic text, or taking the Twelve Steps would never let you down. No! "Your Heavenly Father will never let you down!" he said. As to all of which, Bill Wilson confirmed—underlining in his Big Book the importance of God by saying: "May you find Him now!" At a much earlier date, Wilson had really further *underlined* the necessity for God's help by declaring his thankfulness to the Lord for curing him of his terrible disease, as he explicitly put it (Big Book, 4th ed., p. 191).

All the foregoing contributing elements must also be viewed in the backdrop of A.A.'s qualified teachers of the Word of God, its skilled medical people who oversaw the early experiments, and the drunks who worked with, and helped each other throughout.

You simply cannot discount the necessity for God's help as early AAs in Akron cried out to Him for relief. There was talk of Almighty God at every turn. AA pioneers in Akron were required to believe in the Creator. They were required to accept Christ. They were required to study the Bible and pray. They were required to shoot for a new, Godly life. They were required to help, and witness to, new people. And they were *instructed* in the religious arena by their own first-rate non-alcoholic teachers of compassion and extensive education—Anne Ripley Smith (Dr. Bob's wife), Henrietta B. Seiberling (who "called the shots" at many early meetings), T. Henry

The Earliest A.A. Days

and Clarace Williams (in whose home the meetings were held), and the Oxford Group and Christian writers that the pioneers were reading and discussing.

You also cannot discount the medical help and information the pioneers received from skilled medical people—Dr. Bob Smith in Akron and Dr. William Duncan Silkworth at Towns Hospital in New York. And later, Sister Ignatia at St. Thomas Hospital during the 1940's, when she assisted Dr. Bob.

Nor can you ignore the practical input from alcoholics who were getting well in the program as it developed.

Bill Wilson frequently declared that AAs did not "invent" their program; nor did anyone invent it, he said. The AAs borrowed it. And they correctly called *their* "spirituality" reliance on the Creator! They had been told quite clearly they were 100% hopeless apart from divine help. They believed the Creator could and would provide the help they wanted. They believed the Bible truthfully described, and directed them to the necessary relationship with, God and coming to Him through His Son. And they were guided in their life-changing efforts, almost exclusively, by the teachings of Jesus Christ, as set forth in the Good Book.

The Pioneers Could and Did Help Other Drunks to Cure by the Power of God!

The Emergence of the False Doctrine of "No Cure"

Somewhere, sometime (fairly soon after the successes of pioneer A.A. between 1935 and 1938), someone—undoubtedly an unbeliever—began selling the proposition that there was no cure for alcoholism. Worse!—that those in A.A. itself could *not* be cured. Even though many already had been cured—and said so. For A.A.'s Big Book contained one sentence that sold an unsupported canard. Treatment people jumped on the idea. Therapists jumped on it too. The religious let it pass them by, and seemingly ignored the implications. The implications, of course, limited God Almighty! Finally, A.A.'s own literature gratuitously proclaimed, many, many years later:

> It might also be noted that many terms now considered by A.A.'s to be misleading were then used, not only by non-A.A.'s

discussing the movement, but sometimes by *members themselves*: "cure," "ex-alcoholic," "reformed alcoholic." [*DR. BOB and the Good Oldtimers*, p. 136; emphasis added.]

Those "members themselves" (who had stated clearly and positively that they were cured, yet were later accused of misleading) just happened to be the founders of A.A. And who better would know than they themselves whether or not they had been cured. Certainly not the writer of a biography published many years later. Yet the foregoing piece of theological garbage most assuredly gave aid and comfort to the enemy! The real enemy—also called the Adversary! The very Bible which early AAs used and quoted stated:

> Humble yourselves therefore under the mighty hand of God, that he may exalt you in due time: Casting all your care upon him; for he careth for you. Be sober, be vigilant; because your adversary the devil, as a roaring lion, walketh about, seeking whom he may devour: Whom resist, stedfast in the faith, knowing that the same afflictions are accomplished in your brethren that are in the world. But the God of all grace, who hath called us unto his eternal glory by Christ Jesus, after that ye have suffered a while, make you perfect, stablish, strengthen, settle *you*. (1 Peter 5:6-10)

The courage, strength, and power the early AAs had sought and received was knocked out in one blow with the words "NO CURE." And the knockout blow was promptly followed by FEAR. You can hear that fear at meeting after meeting today—fear of "going out," fear of "relapsing," fear of that "first drink," fear of just about anything and everything. But you do not see that kind of talk in the early A.A. stories. They had been cured! By Almighty God! They had merely to look in their Good Book. What's to fear!

> The fear of man bringeth a snare: but whoso putteth his trust in the Lord shall be safe. (Proverbs 29:25)

> For God hath not given us the spirit of fear; but of power, and of love, and of a sound mind. (2 Timothy 1:7)

Keep Them Sick?

One researcher/writer recently reported that today's A.A. had a seventy-five percent *failure* rate. She commented: Who would want

The Earliest A.A. Days

to sign up for surgery that held out the fact that seventy-five percent would die!

The "no cure" doctrine certainly is, by itself, grossly misleading. If there is "no cure," then millions of dollars are being thrown away on research and treatment—an unfortunate situation that is probably the case. Moreover; the "no cure" doctrine probably gave rise to the "diseasing of America," as one modern-day scholar has called it. [See Stanton Peele, *Diseasing of America: How We Allowed Recovery Zealots and the Treatment Industry to Convince Us We Are Out of Control* (San Francisco: Jossey-Bass Publishers, 1995)]. In effect, the battle cry today appears to have been converted from "Keep it simple" to "Keep *them* sick!"

And how very often I have heard *"in* recovery," "no cure,""keep them in fear" talk in A.A. and treatment meetings: "We are not bad people getting good. We are sick people getting well," you hear. That gobbledegook may sound like a winner in promoting self-esteem, but the whole idea that you never get well, are forever sick, are always "recovering," and cannot be cured is just plain awful! What a prescription for life-long bondage—bondage to illness, bondage to treatment, bondage to therapy, bondage to negatives, and bondage to endless sick ideas within and outside of A.A.

Who Sold out on Seeking God's Power?

Who was it, pray tell, that started selling God short in the A.A. market! Who was it that started declaring AAs should be and are "recovering" *forever*! Who was it that started telling sick newcomers in "self-help" support groups that the *solution to life is meetings*! At the beginning, I literally took that one so seriously that I thought I would turn into a pumpkin if I missed even one single meeting in my first ninety days.

Can it be that the Creator has no power when it comes to alcoholism and addiction? Can it be that *Yahweh* is unable to help unless you go to "ninety meetings in ninety days." Can it be that no one can ever "Just say no." Can it be that revolving door treatment, insurance coverage for treatment, endless therapy, and mountains of meetings are the forever plight of the alcoholic and addict? Can it be that people must join one of the hundred-fold self-help fellowships of today and forever keep sharing joyously at meetings that they are a "grateful, recovering, alcoholic" or "grateful" for whatever sickness or sin they have had.

God forbid. The most encouraging language in the Big Book is: "Rarely have we seen a person fail." What happened to that idea? It contained the answer of A.A.'s pioneer believers, whatever anyone may choose to write or believe today.

Was It the Metaphysical Meandering?

Quite a few Christians are condemning A.A. these days because of the "spiritualism" of Dr. Bob and Bill and the so-called "spook sessions" Wilson conducted at his Stepping Stones abode. And they are so adamant in sticking to historical half-truths that you can barely get them to look at the facts. Yes, Dr. Bob took an interest in spiritualism for a time. He was criticized by his friends in A.A., and he ended all this for good. But not so with Bill Wilson.

You can tar and feather A.A. with spiritualism and "spook" stories if you like. And Bill Wilson's frequent experimentation with L.S.D. (in company with his wife, his secretary, his Jesuit sponsor, and other AAs) has done little to attract support for him among the cult-watchers. Morever, Bill's bouts with depression and spiritualism caused many to believe he was totally off the track spiritually. His womanizing and profit-focus in A.A. probably highlighted his carnal side with clarity. But those who focus on these aberrations are really losing sight of the grace and mercy of God that would apply to Bill and any other person claiming, as Bill did, to be a "practicing Christian." On the other hand, there is evidence that all Bill's meanderings, coupled with Bill's devotion to, and labeling of, Professor William James as a "founder" of A.A., have really whetted the enthusiasm of those who have been busy with Christian-bashing within A.A. and those who have, within A.A.,embraced those bizarre "higher powers" of the metaphysical world.

Bill Wilson's wife Lois and her family were Swedenborgians. Lois's father was a Swedenborgian minister. And, according to Bill's wife Lois, and many others, Swedenborgians are not Christians. Bill and Lois were married in a Swedenborgian church. Bill's long-time mentor/hero, Professor William James, was himself much into Swedenborg's mysticism. [For a brief sketch on Professor James, see Louis Menand, *The Metaphysical Club: A Story of Ideas in America.* (NY: Farrar, Straus and Giroux, 2001), pp. 73-95.]

According to Professor Menand, William James received an M.D. from Harvard, never practiced or taught medicine, began teaching psychology, and then switched to experimental psychology and finally philosophy. In the realm of religion, said Menand, William James had a quarrel with principles and practices of Jews, Roman Catholics, and most Protestant denominations. But he had an affinity to Swedenborgian "occult therapy," the existence of an extrasensory realm, the unseen spirit world, spiritualism, hypnotism, experimentation with drugs, and psychical research. All these were, of course, pursuits contrary to the teachings of the Good Book, yet subjects of continuing interest and experimentation by Bill Wilson.

According to Menand, James "found wanting every organized faith he tried, and he ended as a convert to a religion largely of his own invention." Bill Wilson seems to have followed close behind him in those views. In a word, Wilson's own meanderings do closely resemble those of the deceased professor whom Bill had characterized an A.A. "founder." Professor William James was the only person, other than Dr. Carl Jung, specifically identified in the basic text of Wilson's Big Book. It is important to remember Bill's own background as we consider his interest in Jamesian thinking. Wilson characterized himself as a conservative atheist. He never joined a church. He specifically declined conversion to Roman Catholicism. From entries I found in Rev. Sam Shoemaker's personal journals, it appears that Sam was interested in Bill's receptivity to the Episcopal Faith. But nothing seems to have come of that either despite Bill's close friendship with Sam. Bill read and often mentioned James's *Varieties of Religious Experience* and seems later to have favored aligning A.A. with James's "universalism." Bill specifically mentioned such Jamesian mystical expressions as the "fourth dimension" and "spirit of the universe."

Did all these unusual activities by Bill presage the demise of the power of *Yahweh*, the Creator, in Wilson's later A.A. thinking and writing? I do not know. It seems clear to me, however, that Swedenborgianism; Jamesian mysticism, universalism, and self-constructed religion; and some of Bill's hocus-pocus phrases were not consistent with the biblically-oriented, Christian fellowship of Bill's Akron A.A. involvement in his early days with Bob in the mid-1930's.

It is not A.A. "heresy" to claim . . . that God cures alcoholics without a variety of religious experiences, or spiritual experiences, or spiritual awakenings.

I think it important here to point to some proven facts which some might dub A.A."heresies" and which may upset those in "self-help" fellowships who do not know the specifics of early A.A.: (1) I can help drunks and addicts. (2)You can help drunks and addicts. (3) Doctors can help alcoholics and addicts. (4) Ministers, priests, and rabbis can help.(5) Christians can help. (6) Others can help. And have helped. There can be cure. These are not heresies. They are facts. The truth is simple. The Creator, God Almighty—whose name is *Yahweh*, not "Higher Power"—can cure, has cured, and has healed alcoholics. He did so—long before today's "self-help" groups were even the subject of thought by society. For the most part, of course, the help of humans like you and me was also involved.

No less than two thousand years old, the Bible itself spoke clearly about **cure. Cure by Almighty God: Every conceivable kind of cure—blindness, deafness, dumbness, paralysis, lameness, leprosy, etc.**

The Term "Cure" in Early A.A.

Let's again review the specific remarks by and about Pioneer AAs and the cure they had developed:

Bill Wilson said:(1) "Henrietta, the Lord has been so wonderful to me, curing me of this terrible disease, that I just want to keep talking about it and telling people" (*Alcoholics Anonymous*, 4th ed., p. 191). (2) "God knows we've been simple enough and gluttonous enough to get this way, but once we got this way, it was a form of lunacy which only God Almighty could cure" [Dick B., *The Akron Genesis of Alcoholics Anonymous*, 2d ed. (Kihei, HI: Paradise Research Publications, 1998), p. 13].

Dr. Bob said: ". . . [T]his was a man [Bill Wilson] who had experienced many years of frightful drinking, who had had most all the drunkard's experiences known to man, but who had been cured by the very means I had been trying to employ, that is to say the spiritual approach" (*Alcoholics Anonymous*, 4th ed., p. 180). "Nineteen years ago last summer, Dr. Bob and I [Bill Wilson] saw him (Bill D.) For the first time. . . . Straightaway, Bob called Akron's City Hospital and asked for the nurse on the receiving ward. He explained that he and a man from New York [Bill Wilson] had a cure for alcoholism" (*Alcoholics Anonymous*, 4th ed., p. 188).

Bill Dotson [A.A. Number Three] said: "That sentence, The Lord has been so wonderful to me, curing me of this terrible disease, that I just want to keep telling people about it,' has been a sort of golden text for the A.A. program and for me" (*Alcoholics Anonymous*, 4th ed., p. 191).

Clarence Snyder [who got sober in February, 1938; was one of A.A.'s 40 "pioneers;" and was sponsored by Dr. Bob] said: (1) As to a conversation between Cleveland A.A. Abby G. and Bill Wilson, that Abby had challenged Bill to talk about "this cure, this group of rummies," as to which Abby himself said, "I wanted to know what this was that worked so many wonders, and hanging over the mantel was a picture of Gethsemane; and Bill pointed to it, and said, 'There it is.'" [*Alcoholics Anonymous*, 3rd ed., pp. 216-17; Mitchell K., *How It Worked: The Story of Clarence H. Snyder and The Early Days of Alcoholics Anonymous in Cleveland, Ohio* (NY: A.A. Big Book Study Group, 1997), pp. 138-39]. (2) To his sponsee Mitch K, "I was told that if a rummy wanted what I had, I was to tell them about, and introduce them to that Power greater than myself. The same Power Dr. Bob had introduced him [Clarence] to. The same Great Physician, Dr. Silkworth had told those alcoholics who were declared hopeless could "cure" them. That Power, that Great Physician, was the Christ--Jesus" (Mitch K., *How It Worked*, p. 6, and also pp. 71, 138, 157).

The Rev. Dr. Dilworth Lupton [Pastor of the First Unitarian Church in Cleveland] said: (1) To Dorothy Snyder, wife of Clarence Snyder, that he "thanked Dorothy for her continued interest in his meeting with her husband and for her desire for him [Lupton] to see this new 'cure' in action" (Mitch K., *How It Worked,* p. 156). (2) To the Cleveland Plain Dealer on November 27, 1939, in his article titled "Mr. X and Alcoholics Anonymous," which printed Lupton's sermon concerning this new 'cure.'" (Mitch K., *How It Worked*, p. 157).

Larry Jewell [who was sponsored by Dr. Bob Smith and Clarence Snyder] wrote the following in a series of articles in *The Houston Press* in 1940. [Note that *The Houston Press*'s own editorial preceding the Jewell articles—said, "They [the AAs] say their cure works. They show as witness hundreds of lives restored to health and usefulness, hundreds more among their families relieved or terror and despair, and restored to happiness through the alcoholics' changed lives."] In his six articles, Larry Jewell wrote: (1) "I have personally met at least one hundred 'cured' alcoholics—'fellow rummies' as they jokingly call each other." (2) "Some of the experiences of these 'cured' alcoholics will enliven the serious business of these articles." (3) "You need not buy the book [*Alcoholics Anonymous*] if an alcoholic cured by, and experienced in, the technique of Alcoholics Anonymous will clearly give you an idea." (4) [An artist said]: "It has cured me of a vicious habit." (5) "If wishes were horses, beggars would ride; and the alcoholic could come into his cure on the gallop." (6) "The alcoholic who is following the procedure here outlined begins his day by making conscious contact with this Power—with God. Some call it prayer. Some call it meditation. Some read the Bible. But all of them try honestly to square off the day in the presence of God." (7) "The Houston Press has providentially done a real service to this city by publicizing this cure."

Theodore English [who wrote the following in Scribner's Commentator, in January, 1941] said: (1) "The cure is not medical, but spiritual." (2) "Bill [Wilson] has outlined the cure in twelve specific steps which contain four major points. . ." (3) "People who have been cured find the best insurance—and sometimes the only way to avoid a 'slip' is to help someone else." (4) "The growth of the Houston group is an example of how members have enlisted half the alcoholics they have encountered and cured two-thirds of them through patience and sympathetic assistance."

A physician—an A.A. old-timer—was healed in A.A. and wrote in his personal story "Physician, Heal Thyself": "I couldn't practice medicine without the Great Physician. All I do in a very simple way, is to help Him cure my patients. . . . What is this power that A.A. possesses? This curative power? . . . To me it is God" (*Alcoholics Anonymous*, 3rd ed., pp. 351-52).

In my recent titles, *Why Early A.A. Succeeded* and *God and Alcoholism*, I have discussed **four others** who have spoken eloquently of A.A.'s cure:

The **first** is **William Duncan Silkworth**, M.D., who wrote the "Doctor's Opinion" in A.A.'s *basic* text. See Dick B., *Why Early A.A. Succeeded: The Good Book in Alcoholics Anonymous Yesterday and Today* (Kihei, HI: Paradise Research Publications, 2001), p. 33; Dick

B., *God and Alcoholism: Our Growing Opportunity in the 21st Century* (Kihei, HI: Paradise Research Publications, 2002), pp. 61-62; Norman Vincent Peale, *The Positive Power of Jesus Christ: Life-Changing Adventures in Faith* (Pauling, NY: Foundation for Christian Living, 1980), pp. 59-63.

The **second** is the person who drafted one of the early proposed covers for the First Edition of Alcoholics Anonymous and said it offered a "cure" for alcoholism. See Dick B., *God and Alcoholism*, p. 60; Mitch K., *How it Worked, supra*, p. 133.

The **third** is **Morris Markey**, whose much-quoted, 1939 *Liberty Magazine* article was called "Alcoholics and God." A bold-faced lead said "Is there hope for habitual drunkards? A cure that borders on the miraculous—and it works." The article quoted Bill Wilson as saying, "I've got religion. . . . And I know I'm cured of this drinking business for good." See Dick B., *God and Alcoholism*, pp. 17-18.

The **fourth** is the famous medical writer **Paul de Kruif** who wrote in A.A.'s own *Grapevine* that "The A.A.'s medicine is God and God alone. This is their discovery. . . . It is free as air—with this provision: that the patients it cures have to nearly die before they can bring themselves to take it." See Dick B., *God and Alcoholism*, p. 17; *Volume II: Best of the Grapevine* (NY: The AA Grapevine, Inc., 1986), pp. 202-03.

Were all these people using "misleading" words! Were all these just blowing smoke? I claim no one would be reading a Bible for help if the Bible told them there was no help. No one would be praying to the Creator for healing if the Creator said He was powerless! No one would care to learn about Jesus Christ if Scripture told people that Jesus never healed; never raised anyone from the dead; never cured the deaf, dumb, and blind; and was absolutely powerless to cast out evil spirits and heal lepers and the mentally ill. The Bible says otherwise. See Matthew 9:18-35; 10:1,8; 11:4-5; 12:22; 20:30-34. Only when some in A.A. the treatment industry, or perhaps the insurance industry decided that long-term sickness was in vogue did people seem to begin discounting the power of God and the early A.A. miracles.

There Were Many Specific Cures of Alcoholics before A.A. Began

There certainly were those, immediately preceding and contemporaneous with, A.A.'s founding—people in the Oxford Group—who quit drinking permanently. [E.g., Rowland Hazard (see *Pass It On.*, pp. 113-14); F. Shepard Cornell and Cebra Graves (see *Pass It On*, pp. 113, 116); Charles Clapp, Jr. (*The Big Bender*); Victor C. Kitchen (*I Was a Pagan*); James Houck, Sr., (see Wally Paton, *How to Listen to God*, pp. 73, 90, 96, 99); Russell Firestone (see James Newton, *Uncommon Friends*); and many in Rev. Sam Shoemaker's circle who were well-known at that time.] They were cured. They relied on Almighty God. And they said so! They had no connection whatever with the non-existent A.A. Instead, they attained and maintained quality sobriety and Christian beliefs, practices, and principles for life. Most were, in fact, part of the inspiration for A.A. itself. Bill Wilson often said so.

Give us all a break. Almighty God was in the healing business for centuries before anyone ever heard of a Big Book. That is why Bill Wilson himself wrote: "We have no monopoly on God" (Big Book, 4th ed., p. 95). And A.A. does not!

"Once an Alcoholic, Always an Alcoholic"?

Bill Wilson wrote in the Big Book:

> We have seen the truth demonstrated again and again: "Once an alcoholic, always an alcoholic." Commencing to drink after a period of sobriety, we are in a short time as bad as ever. If we are planning to stop drinking, there must be no reservation of any kind, nor any lurking notion that someday we will be immune to alcohol (Big Book, 4th ed., p. 33).

True or false? Can the "real," "cured" alcoholic drink again with impunity? If he can, was he *really* an alcoholic? If he cannot drink again with impunity, was he *ever* cured? How do you reconcile "cure" with a doctrine of abstinence? Not picking up the first drink—ever—is doctrinal in A.A. So what do you say to the idea of cure? We will revisit the question later. There are significant answers. But first, more background to cover.

2
Let's Use Simple Words That People Understand

We Will Understand "Cure" Best When We Say "Cure"

I think most of us start learning to speak by hearing simple words we understand. Words like "No!" "Mom." "Grampa." "Eat." "Milk." These words start us off even if we do not pronounce them too well at the beginning. Then some tougher words are interjected. "School." "First Grade." "Reading." "Recess." "Baseball." And, however we learn them, we acquire them and use them rather soon. Later "Arithmetic." "Chemistry." "History." "English." And so on. We probably seldom use the dictionary to look up the meaning of these words, and we do not do too badly in understanding them.

Now Bill Wilson had a good education. He went to law school. He traded in the securities market. And his writing and grammar show that he knew how to use words precisely, put sentences together properly, and employ language that at least he, and apparently his peers, understood quite well. When he said he was "cured," Bill knew what he meant. When he said the "Lord" cured him, he knew what he meant. So did Dr. Bob Smith.

Dr. Bob had received extensive religious training as a youngster. He had gone to excellent schools and universities. And he had a medical degree. When he said that he and Bill had found a "cure" for alcoholism, he knew what he meant. When he said "Your Heavenly Father will never let you down," he knew what he meant. And when Bill Dotson, the Akron attorney, said that Bill's remark about being "cured" had become the golden text of A.A. for him, he knew what he meant. When he said he had found God, he knew what he meant.

Let's move forward. The founders explicitly used the word "cure." They often spoke of themselves as "ex-alcoholics." Frank Amos called them "reformed alcoholics." And no one had any doubt what these things meant. Wilson then wrote a textbook which said the pioneers had "recovered." It said they had been considered "medically incurable." It said they were told they were 100% hopeless apart from divine help. And it said they believed that "probably no human power could relieve them of their alcoholism." We doubt there was much dispute over the idea that they had "recovered" by 1937 since most had been bone dry for two years. We doubt they denied they had been "medically incurable," because most of them had been told that by their doctors. It also seems clear they understood what 100% hopeless had meant, because they had been there. Also, "Divine Help," because they prayed to the Creator many times each day.

"Cure" Means Cure!

If you or a loved one is diagnosed with cancer, you are looking for a cure. Not "recovery." Not "remission." Not "treatment." Just plain "cure," whether you can find one or not. So too with AIDS. So too with a stroke. So too with mental illness. And so too with a broken leg. It is cure you want, cure you seek, and cure you claim if your cancer is gone, your AIDS is no more, your stroke has left no disability, you are thinking with reason, and your broken leg is whole. You do not claim a cure if you still have the symptoms; nor if you still have the pain; nor if you still are disabled; nor if you are still looking for treatment. You are cured or you are not. And maybe today, a dozen contributing factors and causes are involved in the disease or malady itself; but you either still have it, or you do not.

The "Dictionary Definition" of "Cure"

Merriam-Webster's Collegiate Dictionary, Tenth Edition, gives several definitions of "cure." It defines the noun "cure" as a spiritual charge, recovery or relief from a disease, something (as a drug or treatment) that cures a disease, a course or period of treatment ("take the cure for alcoholism"), a complete or permanent solution or remedy, and a process or method of curing. The definition of the verb

Let's Use Simple Words That People Understand 21

"cure" is more emphatic: "to restore to health, soundness, or normality; to bring about recovery from; to deal with in a way that eliminates or rectifies; to free from something objectionable or harmful . . ."

Bill Wilson said that A.A. Number Three walked from the hospital a free man, never to drink again. Wilson said of himself that the Lord had cured him. Dr. Bob said they had found a cure. To those three well-educated men, cure meant cure. They were not "recovering." They were not "in recovery." They had been relieved of their alcoholism—freed! Cured!

The Bible—the Source of A.A.'s Basic Ideas—Defines "Cure"

Let's look at some verses from the King James Version that early AAs studied:

> And he [Jesus] said unto them, Go ye, and tell that fox, Behold, I cast out devils, and I do cures to day and tomorrow . . . (Luke 13:32).

> And in that same hour he [Jesus] cured many of *their* infirmities and plagues, and of evil spirits; and unto many *that were* blind he gave site. Then Jesus answering said unto them, Go your way, and tell John what things ye have seen and heard: how that the blind see, the lame walk, the lepers are cleansed, the deaf hear, the dead are raised . . . (Luke 7:21-22).

> Then he [Jesus] called his twelve disciples together, and gave them power and authority over all devils and to cure diseases. And he sent them to preach the kingdom of God, and to heal the sick (Luke 9:1-2).

> Jesus saith unto him, Rise, take up thy bed, and walk. And immediately the man was made whole, and took up his bed and walked: and on the same day was the sabbath. The Jews therefore said unto him that was cured, It is the sabbath: it is not lawful for thee to carry thy bed (John 5:8-10).

Greek Words Translated "Cure" in the King James Version New Testament

A good Bible dictionary is all that is needed to see that the Greek words translated as forms of the English word "cure" in the King James Version have the same basic meaning as the English word "cure" we are discussing in this book:

> CURE (Noun and Verb) **A. Noun.** *IASIS* . . . , a healing, a cure . . . is used in the plural in Luke 13:32; in Acts 4:22, "healing;" in 4:30 with the preposition . . . 'unto healing,' translated "heal." See HEALING. **B. Verb.** *THERAPEUŌ* . . . Eng., therapeutics, etc., denotes (a) primarily, to serve . . .; then (b) to heal, restore to health, to cure; it is usually translated "to heal," but "cure" in Matt 17:18; Luke 7:21; 9:1; John 5:10, Acts 18:9, R.V. See HEAL, WORSHIP [*Vine's Expository Dictionary of Old and New Testament Words* (NY: Fleming H. Revell Company, 1981), p. 261].

Additional insight may also be gained by looking at the *New Bible Dictionary's* discussion of the related topic of miracles and healing:

> **V. Miracles and healing** *a. Healing–its meaning.* Healing means the restoration of one to full health who had been ill–in body or mind (or both). . . . the biblical miracles of healing (apart from cases of demon possession) show healing in its primary medical sense of the restoration to normal in cases of organic disease ... *e. Miraculous healing.* A miracle essentially consists of a striking interposition of divine power by which the operations of the ordinary course of nature are overruled, suspended or modified. . . . So far as miraculous healing in Scripture is concerned, the essential features are that the cure is instantaneous . . . , complete and permanent, and usually without the use of means. . . . Divine miracles of healing show no relapses, which typify spurious miracles. . . . *Miraculous healing in the Gospels.* . . . In the combined narrative of the four Gospels there are over twenty stories of the healing of individuals or of small groups. Some were healed at a distance, some with a word but without physical contact, and some with both physical contact and 'means.' [*New Bible Dictionary*, Second Edition. (England: Inter-Varsity Press, 1982), pp. 461-63].

Let's Use Simple Words That People Understand   23

The A.A. Pioneers Were Cured of Alcoholism

So what did "cured" mean in the early A.A. context? Never to drink again? Restored to Sanity? God-conscious? A Spiritual experience? Faith and dependence upon God? A Spiritual Awakening? Reborn? Miracle?

Bill W.'s Endless, Complicated, Big Book Synonyms for "Cured"

In order to learn about "cure" from A.A.'s basic text--the First Edition of which was published in 1939--you have to leap around the Big Book's varied language dealing with the "cure" subject. First of all, that basic text (*Alcoholics Anonymous*) uses many different, and probably conflicting, expressions having to do with the same, original, simple, concept about which the founders spoke when they said they had been cured of alcoholism.

In the recently-published, fourth edition of the Big Book, these expressions include: (a) *Recovered*, p. xiii. (b) *Relieved of the drink obsession*, p. xv. (c) *keeping sober*, p. xvi. (d) *sobered, never to drink again up to the moment of death*, p. xvi, xvii. (e) *permanent recovery*, p. xvii. (f) *got sober at once and remained that way*, p. xx. (g) *re-created their lives*, p. xxviii. (h) *psychic change enabling control of the desire for alcohol*, p. xxix. (i) *entire abstinence*, p. xxx. (j) *miracle*, p. 11. (k) *recovered from a hopeless condition of mind and body*, p. 20. (l) *having had deep and effective spiritual experiences*, p. 25. (m) *having a vital spiritual experience*, p. 27. (n) *having discovered God*, p. 28. (o) *having established a relationship with God*, p. 29. (p.) *obtaining an effective mental defense against the first drink which "must come from a Higher Power,"* p. 43. (q) *having faith and dependence upon a power beyond ourselves. . . which is God*, p. 46. (r) *consciousness of the Presence of God*, p. 51. (s) *God-sufficiency*, pp. 52-53. (t) *conscious companionship with the Creator*, p. 56. (u) *restoration to sanity—our right minds—by God, a "miracle of healing,"* p. 57. (v) *dealing with alcohol by asking the protection and care of God with complete abandon*, p. 59. (w) *having a spiritual awakening*, p. 59. (w) *being relieved of alcoholism by God as they understood Him*, p. 60. (x) *being reborn by a decision that God was going to be our Director, Principal, Father.* (y) *trusting and relying upon God rather than our finite selves*, p. 68. (z) *acquiring faith that*

God can remove whatever self-will has blocked the alcoholic off from Him, p. 71.

Bill supplied a "recovered" synonym or substitute in the Big Book text for every letter of the alphabet. There are many more in the pages of the Big Book text that follow the foregoing pages ending at 71. But nary a one points to what the founders originally said: "I've been cured." Was "cure" too difficult a word to understand? Was the faith of those that fashioned the Big Book, and well as the faith of those who immediately followed the forty A.A. Pioneers, somehow different from that early faith? An impotent, "powerless," ineffective faith of a weaker kind than that of the forty, early AAs?

If faith changed, strange it is that Bill Wilson was still talking, at page 76, about "victory over alcohol." At page 80, still contending that one alcoholic "had to place the outcome in God's hands or he would soon start drinking again." At page 85, boldly asserting that "our new attitude toward liquor has been given us without any thought or effort on our part. It just comes. That is the miracle of it." It seems quite plain that this articulate, well-educated writer with legal training (Bill W.) knew exactly what he claimed when he proclaimed "victory over alcohol." That Bill also knew exactly what he meant when he spoke of "the miracle of it."

To Me, "Miracle" Means "Miracle." Either the Cure Was a Miracle or It Wasn't!

The one who used the "miracle" word was lawyer Bill. In the basic text of his Big Book, Bill used the word "miracle" seven times (Big Book, 4th ed., pages xv, 11, 57, 85, 124, 128, and 151). And there are more "miracle" words in subsequent pages. In the basic text, Wilson used the word "miracles" five times (Big Book, 4th ed., pages 11, 133, 133, 159, 161). And, in his basic text, he used the word "miraculous" three times (Big Book, 4th ed., pages 25, 50, 55). Make it easy on yourself. Turn to Poe's *A Concordance to Alcoholics Anonymous*, p. 493, find, see, read, and establish for yourself the foregoing quotations.

The Merriam-Webster's Collegiate Dictionary, Tenth Edition (cited above) defines "miracle" quite simply: A miracle is "an extraordinary event manifesting divine intervention in human affairs" (p. 742).

The *New Bible Dictionary Second Edition* (cited above) makes God's role quite clear. It says:

> A number of Hebrew, Aramaic, and Greek words are used in the Bible to refer to the activity in nature and history of the living God. They are variously translated in the EVV by "miracles," "wonders," "signs," "mighty acts," "powers." ... The contention that the NT miracles are more credible in the light of modern psychology or psychosomatic medicine leaves out of account the nature miracles such as that at the wedding-feast in Cana and the calming of the storm, the instantaneous cures of organic disease and malformation, and the raising of the dead. There is no *a priori* reason to suppose that Jesus did not make use of those resources of the human mind and spirit which today are employed by the psychotherapist; but other narratives take us into realms where psychotherapy makes no assertions and where the claims of spiritual healers find least support from medical observers (pp 782-83).

God and Alcoholism (my latest title) contains account after account in the Bible and in books by Christian believers that attest to miraculous cures with God's power, including the cure of alcoholism outside the boundaries of Alcoholics Anonymous. [See Dick B., *God and Alcoholism: Our Growing Opportunity in the 21st Century.* (Kihei, HI: Paradise Research Publications, 2002), pp. 14-25, 54-75, 135, 140-43.]

And Dr. Bob read and circulated many of these accounts of, and books on, healings.

Why, Then, Were Miraculous Cures Effected by the Power of God Later Repudiated!

With page after page of proclamations about miracles, and about the power of God, and about the cure for alcoholism, what gave rise to the following conditional and isolated language in the Big Book basic text—a statement that rests on no support from medicine, from religion, from the experiences of the pioneer AAs, or from the true sources of miraculous information in the Bible:

> We have not even sworn off. Instead, the problem has been removed. It does not exist for us. We are neither cocky nor are we afraid. That is our experience. That is how we react so long as we

keep in fit spiritual condition. It is easy to let up on the spiritual program of action and rest on our laurels. We are headed for trouble if we do, for alcohol is a subtle foe. We are *not cured* of alcoholism. What we really have is a daily reprieve contingent on the maintenance of our spiritual condition (Big Book, 4th ed., p. 85; italics added).

As far as I can tell, Dr. Bob never wavered from believing that he had been miraculously cured through the power of God. In fact, he repeated the following story over and over to his A.A. proteges:

"It was about this boy who burned his hand. The doctor dressed it and bandaged it. When he took the bandage off, the boy's hand was healed. The little boy said, 'You're wonderful, Doctor. You cure everybody, don't you?' 'No I don't,' the doctor replied. 'I just dress the wound. God heals it.'" (*DR. BOB and the Good Oldtimers*, p. 229).

Dr. Bob extensively studied, sought, used, and believed in prayer; God's guidance; and God's *spiritual* healing. At one point in his life, he seemed on the verge of a nervous breakdown. Against doctor's orders, he went with Paul S. to see the dean of Bible studies at Wooster College. And there he "was immediately healed," according to Paul S. (*DR. BOB, supra*, p. 308). To Ruth G., wife of Ernie G. of Toledo, Dr. Bob advised: "Give God a chance" and encouraged her to seek spiritual healing (*DR. BOB, supra*, pp. 312-13). He also suggested a spiritual healing (that was successful) for the child of Clarence Snyder's sister-in-law (*DR. BOB, supra*, pp. 313-14). When he was scheduled to do an operation and wasn't sure, he would pray before he started. He said, "When I operated under those conditions, I never made a move that wasn't right" (*DR. BOB, supra*, p. 314). He frequently prayed for different groups of people who requested him to pray for them, according to Bill Wilson (*DR. BOB, supra*, p. 315). In summary, Dr. Bob used simple words and simple approaches when speaking of, and seeking healings by, God.

As to alcoholism itself, in his own personal story in the Big Book, Dr. Bob spoke about his first meeting with Bill Wilson, saying this about Bill's being *cured*:

But this was a man [Bill Wilson] who had experienced many years of frightful drinking, who had had most all the drunkard's experiences known to man, but who *had been cured* by the very means I had been *trying* to employ, that is to say the spiritual approach (Big Book, 4th ed., p. 180; italics added).

The legal eagle, Bill Wilson, was *later* to use dozens of expressions that were confusing and probably contradictory, yet were perhaps synonymous with complete "recovery" as the Pioneers had experienced it. At the beginning of A.A., however, Bill just said: "the Lord has been so wonderful, *curing* me of this terrible disease" (Big Book, 4th ed., p. 191, italics added).

Dr. Bob Smith the physician—equally articulate—had an education at St. Johnsbury Academy and Dartmouth that had involved some twelve years of Greek and nine years of Latin (*DR. BOB and the Good Oldtimers*, p. 228). He also had excellent training in the Bible as a youngster. But he could and did speak plainly and simply about healing, God, and the Bible.

According to A.A. pioneer Clarence Snyder, who was one of Bob's sponsees and got sober in February of 1938:

> If someone asked him [Dr. Bob] a question about the program, his usual response was: What does it say in the Good Book? (*DR. BOB and the Good Oldtimers*, p. 144).

Dr. Bob himself said that A.A.'s old-timers "were convinced that the answer to their problems was in the Good Book" (*DR. BOB, supra*, p. 96). Bob's talk about the Bible was plain and simple.

Dr. Bob's references to the Creator were equally plain and simple. There were those AAs who, in later days, seemed to have invented a concept of a "Higher Power" that, as they understood Him, could be a light bulb or a Third Avenue bus (*DR. BOB, supra*, p. 161). Not so with Bob. According to A.A.'s own literature, "the earliest A.A.'s agree that Bob presented God to them as a God of love who was interested in their individual lives" (*DR. BOB, supra*, p. 110). In the early days, he would ask the new members if they believed in God (*DR. BOB, supra*, p. 144). He would take new men upstairs at the T. Henry Williams home where AAs met and "make them say that they would surrender themselves to God" (*DR. BOB, supra*, pp. 88-89). And that is as clear a reference to *Yahweh* our God—the One who gave us Ten Commandments—as you can make it.

Now, Just What Was This "Alcoholism" of Which They Had Been Cured?

There is the rub. To this day, scholars and scientists still cannot agree on a definition of alcoholism. Which, in turn, leads to disagreement and confusion over "cure." And that quandary is a major subject in my title *God and Alcoholism.* It is enough here to quote a few of the many scholarly definitions of "alcoholism":

- Alcoholism is a disease. E. M. Jellinek, *The Disease Concept of Alcoholism* (New Haven, CN: College and University Press, 1960).

- Alcoholism as a disease is a myth. Herbert Fingarette, *Heavy Drinking: The Myth of Alcoholism as a Disease* (Berkeley, CA: University of California Press, 1988).

- Alcoholism is both disease and behavior disorder. George E. Vaillant. *The Natural History of Alcoholism Revisited* (Mass: Harvard University Press, 1995).

- As drunkenness, it is sin. Martin and Deidre Bobgan, *12 Steps to Destruction: Codependency Recovery Heresies* (Santa Barbara, CA: EastGate Publishers, 1991).

- As excessive drinking, it is a sickness of the soul—a sin sickness. Jerry Dunn. *God is for the Alcoholic.* (Chicago: Moody Press, 1965).

- Alcoholism is self-defeating behavior, psychological dependence, a progressive neurological disease; or has a "confusing variety of usages." Howard Clinebell. *Understanding and Counseling Persons with Alcohol, Drug, and Behavioral Addictions.* Rev. and enlarged ed. (Nashville: Abingdon Press, 1998).

- Alcoholism is a progressive neurological disease strongly influenced by genetic vulnerability. Inherited or acquired abnormalities in brain chemistry create an altered response to alcohol which in turn causes a wide array of physical, psychological, and behavioral problems. Although environmental and social factors will influence the progression and expression of the disease, they are not in any sense causes of addictive drinking. Alcoholism is caused by biochemical/neurophysiological abnormalities that are passed down from one generation to the next or, in some cases, acquired through heavy or prolonged drinking Katherine Ketcham and William F. Asbury with Mel Schulstad and Arthur P. Ciaramicoli. *Beyond the Influence: Understanding and Defeating Alcoholism* (NY: Bantam Books, 2000), p. 46. . . . Forty years of research into the causes of alcoholism and other addictions have led to one conclusion: irresistable craving is a malfunction of the reward centers of the brain involving the neurotransmitters and the enzymes that control them. Genetic research. . .indicates that the malfunction begins in the gene. Psychological and sociological research indicates that the environment can trigger, worsen, or to some degree alleviate the genetic predisposition, but the determining factors are biogenetic and biochemical (Ketcham, *et. al.*, *supra*, p. 76).

For most of us who have plunged too far into the alcohol vat, I believe, "alcoholism" can be summarized in these terms: We drink far too much. We get mentally and physically sick. We get in lots of trouble—of all kinds. Things get worse and worse. And we still do not stop even though we may say we want to. In fact, I believe Bill Wilson's presentation in A.A.'s basic text of his own and other stories covers the waterfront as to our behavior.

If today—as soldiers in the trenches—we get caught up in attempts to define disease, sickness, behavior, genetics, neurology, and sin, we may well ignore the nature of God's healing--by "faith," by "naturalistic" means, by "nature" miracles, and by "signs." [See Sherwood O. Cole. "Don't Disembody Me Just Yet! A Christian Perspective on Our Biological Nature," *Journal of Psychology & Christianity* (Vol. 21, Summer 2002), pp. 151-60; *New Bible Dictionary*, 2d ed. (England: Inter-Varsity Press, 1987), pp. 457-64,

782-84, 1111.] Those who say that A.A. is a "spiritual" program are not far from wrong if they really mean—as I do—a program whose heart requires reliance on the Creator (trust in God)—as Bill said it did (Big Book, 4th ed., p. 68). But those who focus on questions of disease, genetics, and neurology, seem rarely to talk about God's place in healing. The same when they talk about "behavior." The more people talk about behavior disorder, the less they seem to talk about God's commandments concerning "bad" behavior, the importance of a rebirth, and the availability of (in fact, necessity for) His help in turning the corner. Finally, those who talk about "sin" are often more adamant in their condemnation of it than they are in their compassion for the "sinner's" need for redemption and then for living by God's rules.

Undue focus on disease has promulgated language such as "powerless"—a word that certainly confused me, since I was relying on the *power* of God. Undue stress on "obsession" and "allergy," moved me farther from cure by God. The words suggested a belief that "cure" is beyond the body's own potential. "Progressive" I could relate to. That meant "worse and worse."

But today's extended definitions are not for me. People say, "No cure." Or, "Relapse is OK"—probably meaning inevitable. Or, "Once an alcoholic, always an alcoholic." Not for me! No, thank you! I am long past the point of buying those phrases whole cloth. I am cured. Like Dr. Bob, I do not think relapse is OK. And I do not accept the bondage of being an alcoholic forever. Furthermore, the so-called A.A. miracle seems quite clearly to have taken place for me. I do not want to drink. I have not had a drink. I do not need to drink. I have not had to drink. I do not intend to drink. Life's just too good. And liquor's too bad for me. That is just, plain, "sane" thinking—fostered by my own experience and the thinking I harbored *before* I had "recovered," been "relieved," been "freed," and was cured—with the help of Almighty God.

I do not think you need to define the elements of a miracle. A miracle is a miracle. Again: a miracle is a miracle. Also, I do not think you need to define a cure. An end to a miserable, self-defeating behavior pattern and a horrible life is a cure. I am sure you do not need to define God. You can read all you want to read about Him in the Bible, starting with Genesis 1:1.

Odd, perhaps, but the old Oxford Group formula seems quite relevant. "Sin" (drinking, drunkenness, and certain disaster—for the alcoholic) is the problem. "Jesus Christ" (the power received from God—by reason of Jesus's accomplishments—when we are born again of God's spirit and are *in* Christ) is the "solution." And the "result" is a "miracle." [See H.A. Walter, *Soul-Surgery* (New Britain, CT: Association Press, 1919), p. 128; and Harry Almond, *Foundations for Faith* (London: Moral Re-Armament, 1975), pp. 1-17.] Whether you call "Sin-Jesus Christ-Miracle" a Frank Buchman solution, a Moral Re-Armament solution, "Oxfordization," "old fashioned prayer," true sonship and fellowship with the Creator, or Christian healing, you can use that formula for understanding. Drinking *is the problem* for those of us who commit the sin of drunkenness, contract the disease of excessive drinking, or engage in all sorts of self-defeating behavior that seems to accompany the drunk wherever he goes, no matter who he is. For me, Jesus Christ was "the solution"—asking God for help in the name of His Son Jesus Christ. This petition to the Creator enabled me to overcome "alcoholism" and hence be cured. The result has truly been a miracle. I never expected to be this solid in my relationship with *Yahweh*. I have never been so dedicated to the Bible as the source for truth. I have never been so fully persuaded that these came from confessing Jesus as Lord and believing God raised him from the dead. *And* I have certainly come to realize the importance of obeying the principles and practices Jesus defined as "doing the will of the Father"—as well doing and obeying the other commandments of, and from, God.

What, Then, Is the Cure?

The "Cure" for Sin?

Drinking to excess and drunkenness is sin (Ephesians 5:18—"And be not drunk with wine wherein is excess; but be filled with the Spirit"). God's solution was to deliver us from the power of darkness (Colossians 1:13—"Who [the Father] hath delivered us from the power of darkness, and hath translated *us* into the kingdom of his dear Son"). The cure is found in the miracle of using God's power and our own will to end the drunkenness and, in fact ending it—for good.

The "Cure" for Disease?

Some still insist that alcoholism is a sickness or disease. If so, then asking God in the name of Jesus Christ to heal that disease, believing it can be done, and experiencing its removal *is* the cure. See Acts 3—"In the name of Jesus Christ of Nazareth rise up and walk" (v. 6). ... "And he leaping up stood, and walked, and entered with them" (v. 8). ... "And his name [the name of Jesus Christ] through faith in his name hath made this man strong. ... yea, the faith which is by him hath given him this perfect soundness in the presence of you all" (v. 16).

The "Cure" for the Behavior Disorder?

More and more people are stating that alcoholism is a behavior disorder. If so, then putting your trust in God and walking in His ways *is* the cure (Proverbs 3:5-6--"Trust in the LORD [*YHWH*, Yahweh] with all thine heart; and lean not unto thine own understanding. In all thy ways acknowledge him, and he shall direct thy paths").

The "Cure" for Evil Spirits?

What if there have been evil spirits preventing the cure? These can be discerned by revelation, cast out in the name of Jesus Christ, and overcome in the future by submitting to God and resisting the devil (See 1 Corinthians 12:10—". . . the working of miracles; . . . discerning of spirits"; Mark 16:17—"In my name shall they cast out devils"; James 1:12—"Blessed is the man that endureth temptation: for when he is tried, he shall receive the crown of life, which the Lord hath promised to them that love him"; and James 4:7—"Submit yourselves therefore to God. Resist the devil, and he will flee from you").

I Am Not Mis-applying the Word "Cure"—Just Pointing to the Power of God

There is nothing new in the foregoing verses—nothing that the early AAs could not and did not find in their Bibles and in their topical Bibles such as *The Runner's Bible*. If any or all of the foregoing—sin, disease, behavior disorder, evil spirits—are the problem, then

Let's Use Simple Words That People Understand

believing the Word of God and acting accordingly, will produce the "cure"—the answer, the recovery, the deliverance that is sought (1 John 5:14-15—"And this is the confidence that we have in him, that, if we ask anything according to his will, he heareth us; And if we know that he hear us, whatsoever we ask, we know that we have the petitions that we desired of him").

When Dr. Bob said that A.A.'s old-timers believed that the answer to their problems was in the Good Book, those Pioneers gave every evidence of applying the same Scripture we have quoted above. And their cures were astonishing, miraculous, and accomplished by those who had gone to the maximum in attaining their objectives: to quit drinking, to trust in God, and to walk according to His commandments in the Bible.

These facts as to how God helped early AAs are for you! You can learn our history and help anyone who truly wants to quit drinking and to live an abundant life as Jesus Christ came to make possible for those who believe (John 10:10b—". . . I am come that they might have life, and that they might have *it* more abundantly").

There are, no doubt, statistics galore these days which can, and probably do, "prove" that anyone, just anyone, can quit drinking for good. And that they can and do quit without A.A., without the Bible, without becoming a Christian, and without relying on Almighty God. But the message here involves much more than quitting drinking. It asks: "How were things going when you were self-destructing?" "What were you doing or able to do about the situation by yourself?" "What's so difficult about trusting God?" "How is your life today?" "If you quit on your own, what will be your message for others?"

The "cure" I am describing in this title is simply "old-school" A.A., plus its original firm belief in the way, the truth, and the life (John 14:6—"Jesus saith unto him, I am the way, the truth, and the life: no man cometh unto the Father, but by me"). That "old school" A.A. way works! There was and is a cure. "Old school" A.A. provided *the* way, the path, to a complete cure.

Why was early A.A. described as a Christian Fellowship? Because the foregoing were beliefs studied and firmly held by its members. And, if some of the guides in this title are followed, I believe still more "miracles" will follow. The cure can and will, I believe, be accompanied by a full and abundant life; by fellowship with like-minded believers; by fruitful, Godly service and endeavors; by love for God and His kids, and by a prosperous and healthy life.

3
Newcomer Netting

A Life and Death Matter, As A.A. Sees It

You are not in A.A. long before being indoctrinated with the idea that "working with others" is a "must." Early on in the Big Book, Bill Wilson wrote:

> Our very lives, as ex-problem drinkers, depend upon our constant thought of others and how we may help meet their needs (*Alcoholics Anonymous*, 4th ed., p. 20).

Bill devoted a whole chapter of the basic text to "Working With Others." This service is called "Twelfth Stepping." And Bill's description of it begins:

> Practical experience shows that nothing will so much insure immunity from drinking as intensive work with other alcoholics. It works when other activities fail (Big Book, *supra*, p. 89).

Dr. Bob put it a little less dramatically and intensely—though his service without charge in assisting over 5,000 men and women to recover emphasizes how strongly he felt about helping others who want and need what we have. In fact, Bill called Dr. Bob the "Prince of Twelfth Steppers," proclaiming that we may never again see such devotion and success. And here's how Dr. Bob modestly described his own work:

> I spend a great deal of time passing on what I learned to others who want and need it badly. I do it for four reasons: 1. Sense of

duty. 2. It is a pleasure. 3. Because in so doing I am paying my debt to the man who took time to pass it on to me. 4. Because every time I do it I take out a little more insurance for myself against a possible slip (Big Book, *supra*, p. 181).

I certainly subscribe to this altruistic theme in A.A. which took its real inspiration from the statement in the Book of James: "Faith without works is dead" (James 2:20; Big Book, *supra*, pp. 88, 14). Added to the "working with others" idea of the Twelfth Step (also called "passing it on"—which was an Oxford Group expression as well) must be the idea of *sharing*. See J. P. Thornton-Duesbury, *Sharing* For a long time, AAs have called this the sharing of "experience, strength, and hope with each other" (Big Book, *supra*, p. xxiv). Their Oxford Group forbears and many AAs today still use the expression: "You've got to give it away to keep it."

And here are my personal experiences with, and thoughts about, the whole process.

The Author's Experience, Victory, and Outreach

My Drunkalog?

I'll not write a conventional drunkalog. If you want drinking stories, you can see many in the movies; you can read still more in books; you can hear hundreds more on audio tapes; and you can hear thousands at meetings. Some are "better" than mine, and some are worse. Here's mine in thumbnail form.

I became *dependent* on sleeping pills at the end of Law School in 1951. I achieved heavy-duty *addiction* to those pills later on. I probably crossed the drinking line into alcoholism about 15 years later. Excessive drinking, mixed with prescription pills, became my obsession. I have had the passing-outs, the blackouts, the broken bones, the car wrecks, the marital troubles, the legal troubles, the unwanted publicity, the grand mal seizures, the trip to a treatment program, the trip to the Bar Association, the trip to the VA psych ward, the brief trip to the state penitentiary, and an even more brief trip to the county jail. Oh, I did not kill anybody, not even myself. But I racked up *all* the usual wreckage connected with alcoholism and drug addiction. And that's that. I am fully qualified—before, during, and presently—in Alcoholics Anonymous.

That is my drinking story—one that left me close to death at age sixty.

Here Was a "New" Idea for Me—Helping Others Without Reward

My first grand-sponsor frequently mentioned in meetings that he was (one more time and again) on the hunt with his "newcomer net." He would also say that working with others in A.A. was "not an option" for him. It was, he believed, a necessity. And, while I later really felt very sorry about his open hostility to the Bible and Bible study in A.A.—a trait that drove some distance between us—I know my enthusiasm, determination, and efforts to help newcomers and sponsor men in the fellowship came directly from his remarks and the example he set. He was a whiz.

However, the willingness to go newcomer netting, and the actual techniques for helping, were my own. They were probably acquired initially when I was in my college fraternity at University of California in Berkeley. For example, in fraternity "rushing" at the beginning of each semester, you would be thrust at some incoming and unknown freshman. You'd have to make him feel at ease, friendly to your overtures, enthusiastic about the rushing process, and desirous of joining your fraternity chapter. There was lots of competition between fraternities in rushing season. And you did not have long to make your pitch. Just about one week (You have got lots more time than that in A.A.). For what it was worth, I learned at Cal to smile at a total stranger, stick out my hand, tell him my name, and welcome him to our fraternity house. I enjoyed it. And that might have been the beginning of my "newcomer fever."

Perhaps I also acquired or learned even more of it in my law office. I had read that you do not sit in your office and wait for the client to be ushered into your hallowed chamber. You get off your rear, walk down the hall, greet the client, and tell that client how "good" it is to see him or her. I had thirty-three years of practice in that realm. But there *was* a payoff in legal fees, just as there was a payoff in the fraternity when it ushered in the new, much-desired "Pledge" [new member]. If your newly acquired Pledge was a "nugget," your fraternity had attained new power and prestige! I might add that we cannot claim any "nuggets" in A.A. or that new power and prestige are acquired by chasing them.

Because A.A. was different. I cannot really say that its entrants are likely to be at the top of the social register when they get to us. A.A. was much connected with the Oxford Group people in the beginning. The Oxford Group espoused a saying that stuck in A.A.: "No pay for soul surgery." (See *DR. BOB and the Good Oldtimers*, p 54.) At first, I did not get the meaning. But after helping hundreds of drunks from detox to their "awakenings," I learned there is no monetary pay, no unending gratitude, and no limitless cooperation from the newcomer in our A.A. rooms. In fact, there is no assurance of any success at all, for you or for him. Some therefore call A.A. a "selfish" program. No pay. Just "self" protection. But that is not my view. I call A.A. and its pre-occupation with newcomers a great and rewarding experience like none I have ever had. In the Boy Scouts, they suggested we help an old lady across the street so that we could turn our Tenderfoot Badge right-side up each day. Though I got my Eagle Scout Badge, I think I probably left more than my share of old ladies standing on the sidewalk. Besides, I did not need their help; and others could help them, I imagined. I am not even sure I stood up for the old or crippled people who entered the street car. Too bad for them, I probably concluded. And, anyway, someone else could stand up and give them a seat.

I'd like to think my greatest joy in Alcoholics Anonymous—my absolute greatest—has been the effort I have expended and do expend to this very day in finding some poor frightened and miserable soul at a meeting, perhaps giving him a hug, and guiding him through the rough spots. Assuming, of course, he wants help and is willing to do whatever it takes to make my help pay off *for him*. That is not a selfish program. I'll debate that to the mat with anyone!

The First Contact

Unfortunately, today's A.A. newcomers come from a wide variety of sources; and they do not always come willingly or with enthusiasm. Some are sent to us by courts and probation officers. Some are hauled to us in vans by treatment programs. Some venture in because a minister, physician, therapist, or counselor may "strongly suggest" the A.A. way. Some are still propelled in our direction by wives, parents,

Newcomer Netting

siblings, employers, partners, and so on. That is usually far different from the early A.A. way as it is described in our "Big Book."

However they get to us, they offer a challenge. At least that is how I saw it. My first grand-sponsor "rushed" me at the end of my very first meeting. He helped me buy a Big Book, wrote his name and phone number in the front, and told me to go to "ninety meetings in ninety days." I have not left A.A. from that day forward, nor have I had a drink. But that is another story.

My approach is this: When I go to a meeting, I seldom spend any time looking up friends or talking to them. I look for the fidgety, uncomfortable, often unkempt soul in the corner. The guy who is fumbling at the literature table, or sitting alone, or looking like he can hardly wait to get out of the room. They're easy to spot. In part because no one else is greeting them, except perhaps the "greeter"—if the meeting has one.

But there is lots to be done right then and there, as I see it. You spot the newcomer, with your net at the ready. You march up to him. You give him your name. My sponsees have often mimicked my next moves: I stick out my hand and say, "Hi. I'm Dick. Welcome to the meeting. Here's my card. Please call me anytime." You probably do not have to ask for *their* name. Usually, they tell you their name in the course of the handshake. If they do not, you ask them for it. In Hawaii, the handshake is something else—something between a many-fingered ritual and an arm twist. Though I have been in A.A. out here since 1990, I still have not mastered the shake. So the newcomer usually helps *me*. After they overcome the shock of seeing an older man who seems to want to get to know them, they get an immediate follow-up from me. There are plenty of options from there on.

If they are stalled at the literature table, you ask them if they have a meeting schedule or a Big Book; and you make sure they have one—all this before the meeting even begins. If they are anywhere near the coffee urn, you ask them if you can pour them a cup [They may not be able to stop shaking long enough to pour their own]. If they are anywhere near one of your friends or even another AA who's just not busy, you introduce the new person around [This makes him feel important—a part of the scene. It makes you feel busy and successful. And it often carries the message to others that they too have a newcomer job to do; and they usually do it well, with an

Hawaiian handshake of their own]. If the newcomer is near the seating area, you invite him to sit with you during the meeting itself.

And there is more still to be done. Before, during, or after the meeting, you ask the newcomer where he lives, how he happened to come to the particular meeting, and how long he has been sober *this time* (That gives him a chance to avoid telling you he has been in and out many times and is trying once again). You congratulate him on whatever good news he brings, even if it has just been a few hours since his last drink. You ask him what he does *when* he has working (Then he does not have to tell you he has just been fired, does not have a job, or is receiving Unemployment). Probably the last thing you would want to do (at that early stage) is ask him about his drinking, his troubles, or any questions he might have. He is new. He is embarrassed. He is uncomfortable. And he did not come for a quiz or for cross-examination. You focus on making him like you, like the fellowship, like the meeting, and like to come again. In fact, you ask him if he has wheels or needs a ride. You should ask him for his phone number because he will be tickled pink if you call him very soon and then encourage him to come with you to the *next* meeting.

And there is more. Some take the new person to the "meeting after the meeting." That "meeting" may be in their car, a coffee shop, a restaurant, or curbside. But I prefer a much more personal effort if it looks to me like the guy is serious about God and serious about getting well. So I ask him if he believes in God—just as Dr. Bob did. They do not run away—contrary to popular myth. I have never had anyone tell me he did not believe in God. They're not looking for an argument. They're looking for a friend. Hopefully, they're also looking for help. And then you ask the new guy if he has any troubles. That one is fun because the usual reply is: "I'm fine." Your response can be: "That's great. Because, when *I* came to A.A., I had the law on me; my wife on me; the tax people on me; my creditors on me; my associates on me;" or whoever else you can truthfully mention. Then the guy starts to open up. You ask him if he thinks he has a drinking problem. Without waiting for the answer, you ask him if he would like to get out of the mess he is in. Once and for all! Without waiting for much of an answer, you tell him it is a tough job; but it can be done with God's help. And only with God's help. You can point to the Steps on the wall or the Big Book where God is mentioned over 400 times, and people are urged to "find Him now!" If you believe the guy is warming up and interested, you can take my approach and use

Newcomer Netting 41

the age-old Oxford Group technique of "sharing." Those people had a life-changing technique, called the Five C's—Confidence, Confession, Conviction, Conversion, Continuance. These filtered into, and became the heart of, the Step program Bill Wilson wrote in 1938. And the first "C" is "Confidence." You gain the new man's confidence—in confidence, with confidence. Here's how I do it.

"Talking Story"

There are lots of strange new expressions and actions for the Mainlander to learn when he comes to Hawaii. Things like the weird handshake I mentioned. Then words like "da kine," "mahalo," "aloha," "brudda," and many more. One is "talking story."

"Talking story" is a term they use in Hawaii. I'd never heard it before. It means, roughly: "chatting, having a personal talk, telling tales, maybe even lying a little." Small talk, perhaps. But "talking story" really means getting personal, getting close, getting into serious gab. To me, in A.A., with a newcomer, it means "sharing."

There is nothing I enjoy more in newcomer netting than saying (after all the meeting prelims are over), "Would you like to join me for coffee?" Or, "May I give you a ride?" Or, "Would you like to talk for a little while?" Or, "Would you like to come over to my house, or over to the back of the room, or to my car where we can talk a little more away from the noise and in private?" Of course, they would—provided they did not come with a buddy, come with or looking for a girl friend, or make some previous commitment!

Alkies love to talk. Especially about themselves, their troubles, their past achievements, and their present misery. Especially to someone who has "been there," who cares, and who seems to want to listen. You can trade them shot for shot. There is nothing you have not done or heard that does not bring them to the conclusion that they are with someone who "knows." When Bill Wilson first talked to Dr. Bob, the very sick Dr. Bob was going to give Bill 15 minutes: "Fifteen minutes, tops." But Wilson chattered on and on, thinking he was really telling Bob some new stuff, both medical and religious. Bob commented later that he had heard it all before. What impressed Bob was that Bill talked Bob's language, really seemed to know what he *was talking about*, and really wanted to give Bob the scoop. The two men talked for about six hours, and A.A. began to be born. One drunk talking to another—with the first one really understanding, caring, and honestly telling it like it is; and the second really being warmed by the whole event.

I believe no family doctor, psychiatrist, psychologist, therapist, counselor, minister, priest, rabbi, teacher, interventionist, or facilitator can even come near the sharing process that occurs when two drunks let their hair down, feel comradeship, and start telling the truth to each other. I sometimes say that this initial process may be the only one in A.A. where people really do tell the truth. They're scared. They're wary. But they sense confidence. They lose their suspicion. And they do not have to tell secrets—yet. They just talk about their drinking, their troubles, and their despair. I will not say what I tell them because it depends on the situation. If they feel you really want to listen, you really only need to start the motor running. The game is not to trap them, cross examine them, accuse them, preach to them, admonish them, correct them, convert them, or sell them. It is to listen. It is to listen in confidence and with rapt attention so that you can gain their confidence and help them if they want to be helped.

Next Comes the Vital "Clincher" in My Outreach

If the new guy has shown real desire to be helped and to follow suggestions, he may ask me to sponsor him. Or he may not even know what a sponsor is. If he does not ask or know, I may ask him if he would like to work with me. But, whatever the next episode, there are two serious points I make right then.

The first is to talk to him about "Step Zero." Are you willing to *go to any lengths*? Are you willing to *do anything to get well*? Are you willing to *do whatever it takes*? He probably will not get the full significance, but he should get the point. If he does not get that point and commit himself, I firmly believe it will not work.

The second point, however, is what separates the sheep from the goats as far as working with me is concerned. I say: I want you to listen carefully. I'll use five words. God. Jesus Christ. Holy Spirit. Bible. Door. If you can accept the first four, we will work together. If you cannot, there is the door. By that, I mean that he wouldn't want to work with me. I explain that there are about a million alcoholics in A.A. in America at any given time. If the new man wants help from an atheist, someone who does not believe, someone of a particular faith or persuasion, someone who does not care about God or the Bible, someone who believes something else like tarot cards or crystals, or someone who has some other religious conviction, he is sure to find some such a person who will sponsor him in A.A. I tell him that. So I am not abandoning him. I am just getting the common ground established or—if he is negative about the Creator—making sure we separate before the guy later backs off because of different beliefs. Again, about the only ones who choose the door are a few Christians who say they'd rather be helped in their church or a church fellowship. And they sure go with my blessing. The others are usually far more focused on being helped right then and there than on raising religious questions.

I am a Bible guy, just like Dr. Bob was. Not an Oxford Group person. Not a church evangelist. I am definitely someone who believes, as Dr. Bob's wife Anne said: "Of course the Bible ought to be the main Source Book of all." [See Dick B., *Anne Smith's Journal, 1933-1939.* 3rd ed. (Kihei, HI: Paradise Research Publications, 1998), p. 60.] I know from my own research and manuscript materials that early A.A. was about the first four items I mentioned—God, Jesus Christ, Holy Spirit, and the Bible. I know it now from 12 years of research. I also know how important these four—God, Jesus Christ, Holy Spirit, and the Bible—were and are for cure and spiritual wholeness. In order for *me* to get well again and stay healthy. And for others who may soon find themselves swamped in the "any god," "meetings, meetings, meetings," and fear gibberish. I also believe that there are very few newcomers who are unwilling to believe—unless you invite them to argue.

I think there is truth in the statement: There are no atheists in fox holes. I know that A.A.'s Big Book mentions the Creator in one way or another over 400 times. That is important to know before you go around getting intimidated by the nonsense that mention of God will scare away the newcomer. I know for sure, from A.A.'s own literature, that Dr. Bob insisted on belief in God, the Christian approach, the guidance of the Holy Spirit, and the study of the Bible. That is important for you to know when some interloper starts claiming the Twelve Traditions forbid mention of Jesus Christ. They do not. They *suggest* that sectarian and denominational talk be avoided. But that does not include religion, church, the Bible, God, or Jesus Christ. All are part of A.A. history and legacy. The historical facts are there. The facts are documented—at least in my published materials. People have just forgotten, ignored, or condemned them. But A.A. was founded on those beliefs, and it had astonishing success when they were adhered to. That is when and how the proven cures occurred. The new guy does not need to accept the facts. But he ought to know about them. The A.A. pioneers did—and they succeeded!

And about the Hottentot?

What about the Hottentot—according to *Webster's*, a member of any of a group of Khoisan-speaking pastoral peoples of southern Africa? What about the atheist? What about the Moslem, Hindu, Buddhist, or the idolater who mouths off at meetings quite frequently that "your higher power can be anything you want it to be?" Today, such people are welcome in America. Even the Hottentots, I imagine, if INS will pass them through. They're welcome in public schools. They're welcome in the Armed Forces. They're welcome in our colleges. They're welcome in public welfare and general relief programs. And they're welcome in A.A. But there is nothing in the origins of A.A. that says A.A. wanted to surrender its program to any of their particular belief or unbelief systems.

Early A.A. developed, used, and tested a Christian technique, a medicine, a cure, that relied on *Yahweh*, the Creator. It even used the text book whose contents had been revealed by the Creator. That textbook was the Bible. Pioneers called it the Good Book. It offered a specific and exclusive way of establishing fellowship and sonship with God—through acceptance of Christ. It provided the way to gain access to the power of the Holy Spirit through a new birth from above. And all were part of A.A.'s own, rich, successful practices, principles, and literature of the early 1930's. In fact, as Bill Wilson once explained to his Roman Catholic friend and editor of two of A.A.'s Conference Approved books (Father John C. Ford, S.J.), it did not matter to Bill what the Buddhists did with the Twelve Steps. If they wanted to be in A.A., or use the Steps, or adapt them, that was their business, Bill wrote. But those facts did not call either for their ejection or condemnation or isolation, *or* for A.A. to re-write its program to accommodate their predilections. Their views and beliefs were simply not to be the subject either of sanction, as the Roman Catholic priest had suggested, or of adoption. Just simply to be ignored and allowing them to live—an A.A. Slogan, by the way ("Live and let live").

But, that was not how Dr. Bob felt about those matters. He was uncompromising when it came to God, Jesus Christ, and the Bible.

But Bill's approach did offer one way of looking at the universalized A.A. of today. I suppose I look at it that way sometimes. I am not there to fight. I came to A.A. bewildered, sick, and aware of my need to overcome drinking. Then, almost immediately, to rely on the care of the Almighty God, *Yahweh*, the Creator. And it is not my privilege, or duty, or mission to change A.A. But it has been my joy and privilege to help many people to quit drinking and using forever. And to suggest they do so by turning to God for healing, forgiveness, and guidance, doing their best to obey His precepts, studying the Bible for His truth, and helping still others to do likewise.

But what about the Hottentot? Or the guy who has heard in meetings that God can be a tree? I just had lunch with an eminent rabbi, who is also medical director emeritus of a well-known treatment center. I asked him what he thought about the statement in A.A. that "your higher power can be a lightbulb or a radiator." He said, "It's not a problem if you're foolish enough to believe it!" His wry smile was enough to suggest we AAs are not about reclaiming fools from their folly.

The Victory

The victory for me, for a believer, and for those who seek God's help, is grace, mercy, and peace from God the Father and Christ Jesus my Lord, and the promise of life which is in Christ Jesus. It is not about drinking or not drinking. In fact, for most of us, things became much worse when we quit. It is about being sick and getting *cured*. It is about having been fear-filled and feeling condemned but then being filled with the spirit of God and knowing for sure that I am God's kid, as Jesus made available and described in John 3:1-16. It is about having been focused, even controlled, by carnal thoughts and possessions instead of living the abundant life Jesus Christ promised in John 10:10. It is about anticipating a mere several earthly decades and winding up in a hole in the ground rather than being gathered together with everlasting life when Jesus Christ returns for the saints as is promised and explained so well in Thessalonians 4:13-18 and elsewhere.

My victory cannot be found in a book, a step, a sponsor, a meeting, or a fellowship. My victory is something God planned, makes available, and provides to those who do—as the early A.A.

pioneers did—come to Him through His Son Jesus Christ. The son who is the way, the truth, and the life.

I have not met an alcoholic who did not want such a victory if he thought it could really be a part of A.A. participation, who believed he could actually obtain it, and was given clear instructions on how to experience it. For the devoted Roman Catholic and the Jew, there may be different paths; but the victory, if attained, comes from *Yahweh*, the Creator. [See, for example, the Roman Catholic Reader's Edition of *The Jerusalem Bible* which quotes "the servant of Yahweh," in a portion of Isaiah 42:1-35, and then points to Jesus as "the servant of Yahweh," quoting the words from Isaiah 42:1-4, in Matthew 12:15-21. See also Kohlenberger's *The Interlinear NIV Hebrew-English Old Testament* setting forth the Hebrew text and its English translation of the same portions of Isaiah (42:1-35) containing *Yahweh* in the Hebrew text. None of this discussion is an attempt to reconcile Protestant, Roman Catholic, or Jewish doctrines. But it does verify that the Bible, for each and every one of those three faiths, was talking about and dealing with the same Creator, *Yahweh*, our God. *Yahweh*—the same, sole, reigning God for Jews, Protestants, and Roman Catholics alike. See also the foregoing verses in *Rotherham's Emphasized Bible* and in *The Scriptures* (published by Institute for Scripture Research, Ltd.)].

Dr. Bob spoke eloquently about feeling sorry for the atheist, agnostic, critic, and so on. His concluding remark to such people was: "Your Heavenly Father will never let you down!" (*Alcoholics Anonymous*, 4th ed., p. 181). I opted to believe that. And that is what you get if you are actually bagged in my newcomer net and are truly willing to love God with all your heart, soul, mind, and strength. That is what the Heavenly Father commands: See Mark 12:29-30; Matthew 22:36-40. And early AAs mentioned those verses quite often.

What Does This Newcomer Stuff Mean to You?

Let's assume first that you are in A.A. or in one of the related "self-help" groups. Do you want to recover or be "in recovery." Do you want to be recovered or be "recovering." Do you want to be well or be sick. Do you want to be healed or be "in treatment." Do you want to be "cured" or just have a "daily reprieve" and avoid drinking one day at a time. Do you want to be delivered or just to wallow in the

Newcomer Netting 47

power of darkness. Do you want to be victorious, an "overcomer," a believer, and a son of God or just be someone who attends meetings regularly, abstains from booze, and hopefully, takes the Twelve Steps. If early A.A. cures are for you, then this newcomer material means something to you.

Let's assume you want to help someone who is in, or perhaps should be going into, A.A. Do you just tell them to go, nag them to go, advise them to go, recommend that they go, or stand back and "detach." Do you merely ask them if they are going to meetings and not drinking. Do you merely tell them they need to go to A.A. for their alcoholism but to church for their religion.

My view is that cure can be accomplished with God. In or out of A.A. In or out of church. And in or out of the doctor's office. My belief is that God can cure alcoholism, that He did cure the founders of A.A., and that He will cure those who become His kids, ask Him for healing in the name of His Son Jesus Christ, believe in His power to do so, obey His commands, and stay in fellowship with Him through actions, study of His Word, prayer to Him, and listening to Him. If you know that early AAs believed these ideas, acted on them, and were cured, you can help someone in or into A.A. You can tell them early A.A. *was* about the power of God—and only about the power of God. You can tell them it *was* about Bible study, prayer, and God's guidance. You can tell them it *had* an astonishing success rate— 75% to 93% among the "medically incurable" alcoholics who "really tried"--in those days. You can tell them they need to find and fellowship with someone in A.A. (if that is to be their destination) who believes those things today. You need to tell them that passing this message along to others who still suffer should be their primary purpose, just as AAs did. You need to tell them it is OK to fellowship with other believers, to stick with your faith without wavering, and to be ambassadors for Christ as the Bible directs (See 2 Corinthians 5:20). You need to encourage them in their reliance on the Creator, to pray for them yourself, and to stand by your own beliefs instead of caving in to some idolatrous "higher power" of unknown origin or meaning.

Learn what A.A. *was.* Learn what early AAs accomplished. Learn that no treatment or therapy or counselor or doctor or psychologist or church or minister or priest or clergy has produced the same success that reliance on God Almighty for cure produced when A.A. first began. You can prove it. The facts are documented. And you will only discredit those facts if you give nodding approval to nonsense gods like a radiator. Or if you invent some self-made religion that merely involves going to meetings. Or if you try to sell some to half-baked prayer that has no foundation in God's will.

Cure is still very much available. Tell it. Believe it. See it! In fact, I very much like the phrasing of a Teen Challenge pamphlet just sent to me by a very sick man who went to them about ten months ago. The pamphlet says: "Teen Challenge Offers the Proven Cure for Today's Drug Epidemic." It goes on say that the Wall Street Journal cited research studies showing Teen Challenge's long-term cure rates as high as 85 percent. Not surprisingly, the "proven cure" rests on acceptance of Jesus Christ, study of the Bible, and relying on the power of God, among other things. Surprise. Surprise. You could have written such a pamphlet in the 1930's about early A.A. About the A.A.. with a success rate that reached 93 percent in Cleveland even in the *early* 1940's. Two years after the publication of Bill's Big Book, Clarence Snyder surveyed all the members in Cleveland. Clarence "concluded that, by keeping most of the 'old program,' including the Four Absolutes and the Bible, ninety-three percent of those surveyed had maintained uninterrupted sobriety" (See Mitchell K., *How It Worked*, p. 108). The newcomer needs to know that. The newcomer needs to turn from fear to what God can do. That is the largest part of newcomer netting—as I like to conduct it. It is proven. It means cure. It definitely involves Almighty God, *Yahweh.*[1]

---

[1] The personal name of the Creator—the God of the Bible--is *Yahweh* ("*YHWH*"—spelled in Hebrew letters). For more information on this vitally-important name, see Dick B., *Why Early A.A. Succeeded: The Good Book in Alcoholics Anonymous Yesterday and Today (A Bible Study Primer).* (Kihei, HI: Paradise Research Publications, 2001), pp. 47-66, 209-23; Exodus 3:15; 6:3; S. R. Driver and Charles A. Briggs, *The New Brown-Driver-Griggs-Gesenius Hebrew and English Lexicon* (n.p.: Christian Copyrights, 1987), p. 217; Everett Fox, *The Five Books of Moses* (New York: Schocken Books, 1995), p. xxix; David J.A. Clines, "Yahweh and the God of Christian Theology," *Theology 83* (1980), pp. 323-30; *New Bible Dictionary*, 2d ed., organizing ed., J.D. Douglas., under "God, Names of, " pp. 429-30; Internet version of the *Encyclopedia Britannica* (http://www.britannica.com/), in its article on "Yahweh"; Kenneth L. Barker, "YHWH Sabaoth: 'The Lord Almighty.'" *The NIV: The Making of a Contemporary Translation* (http://www.gospelcom.net.ibs/niv/mct/9.php). Examples: Jeremiah 32:27, *Jerusalem Bible*; Exodus 6:3, *The Scriptures*. 2d ed. South Africa: Institute for Scripture Research, 2nd. ed, 1998; Exodus 3:15, *Rotherham's Emphasized Bible*. (MI: Kregel Publications, 1994); *Complete Jewish Bible*, translation by David H. Stern. (Maryland: Jewish New Testament Publications, 1998), pp. xxxiii-xxxiv, Exodus 3:15, 6:3.

4
What History Can Teach You in, and about, A.A. Itself

The "Spins" You Need to Ignore

Much of the richness of early A.A. simply vanishes in the "spins" people have put on our history. Purported historians and history buffs talk about the Oxford Group of early A.A. as if that First Century Christian Fellowship was a tool of Adolph Hitler's. And God's guidance as if it were a one-way flow of garbage that contains the good and the bad and has to be sorted out. Worse, they just do not talk about Anne Smith, Sam Shoemaker, Quiet Time, the Bible, or the Pioneers very much at all. You'll have some tell you that all the early A.A. pioneers died drunk. You'll hear or read fabricated meanings for A.A. Slogans that were never a part of the original picture at all. In fact some just re-define even the Four Absolutes to suit their own taste. They talk about "Six Steps" which never existed either in A.A. or in the Oxford Group. They talk about "four steps" which also never existed either in A.A. or in the Oxford Group. They constantly inject idolatry into almost every mention of *Yahweh*, the Creator, calling Him an "it," a "higher power," a "radiator," a "group," "Good Orderly Direction," and many other absurd names. You have heard all this or read it all, if you have been around A.A. very long. And the "spinners" even pervert "God as we understood Him" to whatever meaning anyone—sick or well, stupid or wise—chooses to call Him or to describe His supposed characteristics.

These and lots more "spins." I have covered them many times in my other titles. And this title will simply suggest how people within

A.A., people studying A.A., and people working with AAs, can at least get a handle on A.A.'s early God-centered program and successes if they know their A.A. history. This *presentation* offers just the barest of sketches. I have published eighteen other titles with detailed, documented facts about the early A.A. roots, ideas, practices, and history.

History and the Big Book, A.A.'s Basic Text

Akron's Program Was Biblical.
It Disclaimed the "Oxford Group Connection"

Note this point very carefully. A.A.'s Big Book basic text does *not* contain or describe the early A.A. program. Hardly a word of it. The original program—developed in Akron and described in the Frank Amos reports of 1938—was biblically oriented, consisted of a Christian fellowship, held "old-fashioned prayer meetings," and required confessions of Christ. There were no Steps at all. There were no significant Oxford Group techniques that underlay the program either. And, unlike what Bill later borrowed primarily from Rev. Sam Shoemaker and put together in the Big Book, the Akron program insisted it had no connection—direct or indirect—with the Oxford Group program. Thus, *DR. BOB and the Good Oldtimers* states on page 135, with reference to what Frank Amos found when he investigated Akron:

> He [Frank Amos] also stated that members did not want the movement connected directly or indirectly with any religious movement or cult; they stressed the point that they had no connection whatever with any so-called orthodox religious denomination, or with the Oxford Movement. [Obviously, Amos meant the Oxford Group: the older, Anglican "Oxford Movement" played no part in A.A. history.]

The importance of the foregoing Oxford Group disclaimer is underlined by a personal, handwritten letter written by Dr. R. H. Smith (Dr. Bob) on his letter-head to Bill Wilson on February 17, 1938 following the week-long visit and investigation in Akron by Amos. I have a photo copy of this letter bearing Bob's handwriting and signature. It states in part, as to Frank Amos:

What History Can Teach You in, and about, A.A. Itself 51

> Of course he [Frank Amos] heard some Oxford Group... chatter but we tried to impress him with the fact that as far as the alcoholic setup was concerned we could not be identified with the group and explained why such a setup was impossible. I think he understands things O.K.

In other words, there was Oxford Group chatter in Akron. There was mention of the Four Absolutes, of Guidance, of Restitution, and of the Five C's. But these were not the essence of the Akron program. In fact, the Akron meetings were for drunks—being assisted by T. Henry Williams and a few Oxford Group adherents. Bob E. put it this way:

> Dr. Bob and T. Henry "teamed" the [Wednesday night] meeting; T. Henry took care of the prayers with which the meeting was opened and closed. There were only a half dozen in the Oxford Group [Bob E. said]. We [the alcoholics] had more than that. Sometimes we'd go downstairs and have our meeting, and the Oxford Group would have theirs in the sitting room [*DR. BOB, supra*, p. 142].

Old-timer Annabelle G. noted that she and her husband Wally had read a great deal about the Oxford Group meetings being held at the Mayflower Hotel in Akron. She said that it wasn't until *later* that they realized the meeting at T. Henry's was "sort of a clandestine lodge of the Oxford Group" (*DR. BOB, supra*, p. 121); and Bill Wilson replied to her comment by saying, "That's right. Some of the groupers did snoot the Williamses pretty badly about having those alcoholics."

Bill Wilson's Twelve Step Material, by Contrast, Came Directly from the Oxford Group and Several Other Sources

Bill acknowledged *his own* Oxford Group Twelfth Step borrowing as follows:

> Where did the early AAs find the material for the remaining ten Steps? Where did we learn about moral inventory, amends for harm done, turning our wills and lives over to God? Where did we learn about meditation and prayer and all the rest of it? The spiritual substance of our remaining ten Steps came straight from Dr. Bob's and my own earlier association with the Oxford Groups, as they were then led in America by that Episcopal

rector, Dr. Samuel Shoemaker. [See Dick B., *New Light on Alcoholism: God, Sam Shoemaker, and A.A.* 2d ed. (Kihei, HI: Paradise Research Publications, 1999), pp. 4-7.]

Bill did not begin his Big Book text writing until after the Amos visit. But his interrelationship with Shoemaker in New York had existed from A.A.'s very first days. The Big Book itself was written in 1938, almost exclusively, if not entirely, by Bill Wilson. Its Twelve Steps had not theretofore existed and most assuredly were written by Wilson. Dr. Bob said that he himself had nothing to do with the writing of them. And the personal stories of the pioneers—which were originally intended to be virtually the sole content of the Big Book—were relegated to the back section; and seldom mentioned the Big Book's own program ideas.

The Big Book basic text ideas themselves were obtained from a hodge podge of sources. Bill Wilson virtually said so, though he finally claimed that almost all the Step ideas came directly from Sam Shoemaker. That, I would add, was not far from totally right. The Twelve Steps actually follow a life-changing pattern found in 28 Oxford Group ideas that impacted on A.A. [See Dick B., *The Oxford Group and Alcoholics Anonymous: A Design for Living That Works*. 2d ed. (Kihei, HI: Paradise Research Publications, 1998).] The heart of the Twelve Steps can be found in the very words of Rev. Sam Shoemaker; many of the ideas of Shoemaker and Professor William James; some of the thinking of Dr. William Silkworth; and some of the life-changing techniques of the Oxford Group. The Oxford Group techniques—those *codified* in Bill's book and Steps—consisted primarily of the Group's "Decisions," "Five C's," "Four Absolutes," "Quiet Times," "Two-way prayers," "Guidance," "Surrenders," "Restitution," "Teamwork," plus some other principles taken by the Group directly from the Bible itself.

Identifying Bill's actual and exact sources is quite difficult. First, Bill Wilson left out mention of the Bible, except for a few unacknowledged verses *from* the Bible. Bill left out Jesus Christ—who was the constant subject of mention in the Oxford Group and early A.A. Bill left out all mention of the Holy Spirit. And he adopted some "New Age," "New Thought," and metaphysical ideas he probably acquired from such non-Oxford Group people as Emmet Fox, Ralph Waldo Trine, Charles and Cora Fillmore, Glenn Clark, and others of a still-earlier period of writing such as William James and Henry Drummond. Bill fashioned his own concept of alcoholism—dubbing it a mental, physical, and spiritual malady. And he adapted some medical thoughts from Dr. Silkworth.

Bill did a masterful piece of writing, in my opinion; but he was not describing the program reported out by Frank Amos in 1938. That program, however, is the program that produced the great successes of the pioneer 40.

History and the Twelve Steps

There were no Steps in early A.A. Not one. None at all. There were no Steps in the Oxford Group. Not one. None at all. There were not even the alleged "Six Steps" which are sometimes attributed either to the Oxford Group or to the word-of-mouth efforts of individual AAs, primarily those on the East Coast. Nor were there "Four Steps," as erroneously contended by Oxford Group old-timer James Houck, Sr. (See Wally Paton, *How to Listen to God*, pp. 90, 103; and compare the research and findings by Reverend T. Willard Hunter—an Oxford Group staff member, writer, and historian—as to the supposed but non-existent "steps" of the Oxford Group. *Pass It On*, p. 206, n. 2). And there certainly were no Twelve Steps at all until Bill Wilson wrote them in late 1938. But all the forces and sources mentioned above in connection with the Big Book converge in the Big Book's presentation of the Twelve Steps. And these Steps can best be understood by looking at their historical sources, instead of by adding new interpretations and guides. As Wilson himself so often said: Nobody invented A.A. The ideas were borrowed. Hence it behooves all of us to study and learn specifics about the sources from which Wilson probably gathered and then borrowed his ideas.

Some may disagree with the following presentations concerning a particular Step or all the Steps. They can hardly disagree with the documented sources historically related to the particular Step. In fact, they should be able better to understand and discuss each Step. And there are unusual historical ingredients pertaining to most Steps that can be most helpful to know. The discussion of each Step that you will find in this segment does not purport to quote or even describe the Twelve Steps found in the Big Book. It does not purport to re-write the Steps. I just do not believe that should be done. But it does phrase the step ideas by discussing and adding to them some of their actual historical roots.

First, Bill Wilson knew very little about the Bible at any point He frankly told this to Akron Pioneers T. Henry and Clarace Williams when he interviewed them in 1954. Bill never belonged to or attended church. And his Bible tutoring, such as it was, came largely from his three-month stay with Dr. Bob and Anne Smith in Akron for three months. On the other hand, Bill's basic exposure to the Step ideas came from his close relationship with Rev. Sam Shoemaker in New York and Shoemaker's exposition of Oxford Group principles in that area. Over and over, Bill wrote about the importance of his friendship with Shoemaker and the vital role Shoemaker played in the Twelve Step process. Primarily from these sources, Wilson picked up—whether embodied in his Big Book language, or in the ideas of his Steps—some major ideas about deflation in depth, honesty, confession, life-change, restitution, prayer and "meditation," working with others, and adherence to Christian principles in daily living. As shown, Dr. Bob had nothing at all to do with Wilson's Steps or the writing of the Steps. But Dr. Bob, his wife, and the other Akron pioneers certainly knew the Oxford Group literature, the Bible, and the prayer principles quite well. Bill Wilson said so. Consequently, you can see a few of Bill's deflation of self ideas, a lot of Oxford Group life-changing principles, a spattering of Bible ideas (that probably came from the Akron crew), and the Oxford Group teachings of Shoemaker mixed together in Bill's Twelve Step discussions.

But, to attempt finding a theology or consistency in the Step process, from a Christian standpoint, is not possible. See Martin and Deidre Bobgan. *12 Steps To Destruction: Codependency Recovery Heresies* (CA: EastGate Publishers, 1992); Cathy Burns. *Alcoholics Anonymous Unmasked: Deception and Deliverance* (PA: Sharing, 1991). You can, however, flavor your understanding of the Steps as Wilson saw them, and perhaps can avoid a good deal of the later absurdity, idolatry, self-made gods, and religion. My titles spell out in detail and extensively document the ideas that are simply sketched below.

An Historical View:
Twelve Steps and Their Main Roots

Let's take a quick look to see what historical material can be of use in helping the alcoholic who chooses to add A.A.'s spiritual, Oxford

What History Can Teach You in, and about, A.A. Itself   55

Group, and biblical history to his Twelve Step thinking. The presentation comes from some of the early language used, primarily by Bill, in connection with each of Bill's Step ideas.

One: We admitted we were licked. Alcohol was our master. We prayed: "O, God, manage me because I can't manage myself."

[For the "licked" idea, see *Alcoholics Anonymous Comes of Age* (NY: Alcoholics Anonymous World Services, Inc., 1957), p. 160; Richmond Walker. *For Drunks Only* (MN: Hazelden, n.d.), p. 23. For the "alcohol was our master" idea, see Big Book, 4th ed., page 8; Victor Kitchen, *I Was a Pagan, supra,* p. 67. For the "O, God, manage me" prayer, see Dick B., *Anne Smith's Journal, 1933-1939.* 3rd ed.(Kihei, HI: Paradise Research Publications, 1938), pp. 20-21; A. J. Russell, *For Sinners Only* (London: Harper & Brothers Publishers, 1932), p. 62; and Peter Howard, *Frank Buchman's Secret* (New York: Doubleday & Co., 1961), pp. 41-44.]

Two: We became "willing to believe" that God could cure us; to "act as if" He would; and to take the action that proves God really can and does cure.

[For the "willingness to believe" idea, see John 7:17 and Shoemaker's many explanations of that idea. Samuel M. Shoemaker, *Religion That Works* (NY: Fleming H. Revell Company, 1928), p. 58. For the "act as if" idea, see the *Readers Digest* article by Sam Shoemaker by that title. For "acting" on Bible ideas, see James 1:22: "But be ye doers of the word, and not hearers only, deceiving your own selves"—a verse often quoted by Rev. Shoemaker. Samuel M. Shoemaker. *The Gospel According to You* (NY: Fleming H. Revell, 1934), pp. 46-47.]

Three: We "made a decision" to "rely on the Creator" for help and to "do His will."

[Rev. Sam Shoemaker frequently said, as to the necessity for "self-surrender," that it must begin with a "decision." Samuel Shoemaker. *National Awakening* (NY: Harper & Brothers, Publishers, 1936), pp. 52-53. For the "reliance on our Creator" idea, see Big Book, 4th ed., p. 68. For the necessity to "do" God's will, see Jesus's sermon on the mount: Matthew 6:10—"Thy will be done"; and Matthew 7:21: "Not everyone that saith unto me, Lord, Lord, shall enter into the kingdom of heaven; but he that doeth the will of my Father which is in heaven." And you often find "Thy will be done" in Bill Wilson's writings, Big Book prayers, and the "Lord's Prayer" that concludes most meetings.]

Four: We gave ourselves a written, moral test, checking our life by the "four absolutes"--the standards of God's will taught by His Son Jesus—honesty, purity, unselfishness, and love.

[For the idea of "making the moral test," see Dick B., *Anne Smith's Journal, supra*, p. 32. For the idea of "writing down the review and putting down everything that does not measure up," see Shoemaker's *How to Become a Christian* (NY: Harper Brothers, 1953), pp. 56-57. For the four "Absolute" standards themselves, see Robert E. Speer's *The Principles of Jesus* (NY: Fleming H. Revell Company, 1902). For the biblical root of the self-examination idea—in a section of the sermon on the mount that was much quoted, see Matthew 7:1-5: "Thou hypocrite, first cast out the beam out of thine own eye; and then shalt thou see clearly to cast out the mote out of thy brother's eye." Samuel M. Shoemaker. *God's Control* (NY: Fleming H. Revell, 1939), p. 63.]

Five: We admitted our moral failures to God, to ourselves, and to another believer.

[For the "confession" aspect, see James 5:16. Samuel M. Shoemaker. *The Conversion of the Church*, p. 35. For the language, "admitting to God, to ourselves, and to another believer," see Dick B., *Anne Smith's Journal, supra*, pp. 39-40.]

Six: We became "convicted" of sin against God; were "willing" to "hate and forsake" the sins uncovered, and to ask that God "remove those sins" from our lives.

[As to "conviction of sin," see Walter, *Soul-Surgery, supra*, pp. 97-116; Samuel M. Shoemaker, *Realizing Religion* (NY: Association Press, 1923), pp. 21, 81-82. As to acknowledging guilt for sinning against God, see Harold Begbie, *Life Changers* (NY: G. P. Putnam's Sons, 1927), p. 169; Psalm 51:4—"Against thee, thee only, have I sinned, and done *this* evil in thy sight. . . ."As for repentance and "willingness" to "hate and forsake" the sin, see Almond, *Foundations For Faith, supra*, p. 6; Samuel M. Shoemaker, *National Awakening* (NY: Harper & Brothers, 1936), p. 58; *Confident Faith* (NY: Fleming H. Revell, 1932), p.117; *The Gospel According to You* (NY: Fleming H. Revell, 1934), p. 113. As to God's "removal" of the sins, see Dick B., *Anne Smith's Journal, supra*, p. 47; Victor C. Kitchen, *I Was a Pagan* (NY: Harper & Brothers, 1934), pp. 143, 180; and Psalm 65:3—"Iniquities prevail against me: as *for* our transgressions, thou shalt purge them away."]

Seven: We "humbled ourselves, submitting ourselves to God;" were "born again" of His spirit and therefore became a "new creature in Christ;"could thereafter be renewed in the spirit of our mind; and could put on the new man which is created in righteousness.

[It seems very probable that "conversion," of which both Dr. Carl Jung and Bill W., spoke, was part of the Seventh Step idea; but the theology of the language is difficult to understand. From his earliest writings, Sam Shoemaker spoke of "conversion" and "self-surrender" in the same breath. See Dick B., *New Light on Alcoholism: God, Sam Shoemaker, and A.A.*, 2d ed. (Kihei, HI: Paradise Research Publications, 1999), pp 107-16. See particularly,

Shoemaker's *Realizing Religion, supra,* which is discussed at length in *New Light on Alcoholism.* Shoemaker also spoke a great deal about "being born again." See *New Light on Alcoholism, supra,* pp. 92-97. But the biblical requirements of John 3:16 and Romans 10:9 are missing from the A.A. language that emerged in Bill's Seventh Step. However, the concept of James 4:10—"Humble yourself in the sight of the Lord"—seems involved (but again, Jesus is not mentioned in the relevant A.A. text). "Submit yourselves therefore to God"—from James 4:10—also seems to be involved in Bill's self-surrender idea. And that verse was quoted frequently in the materials Dr. Bob studied, but little mentioned in Shoemaker's writing. "Ye must be born again"—from John 3:7—can be seen over and over in Shoemaker and Oxford Group writings. But "salvation" (as a word) seemed to be a "no no" subject except for Buchman and his closest adherents. Finally, the idea of a "new creature in Christ"—from 2 Corinthians 5:17—was often quoted in the Oxford Group and by the Akron AAs. And, whatever the language of the Big Book itself; it seems fair to say that all the foregoing Scripture really did really produce among early AAs the belief: (1) That their past sins were blotted out through the redemption that is in Christ Jesus (Romans 3:20-30; Colossians 2:13-15); (2) That, as believers, they had been "transformed"—made complete in Christ—and been delivered by God from the power of darkness and translated into the kingdom of His dear son (Colossians 1:13-14, 2:7-10); and (3) That they now had access by one spirit unto the Father, *Yahweh.* (Ephesians 2:18).]

Eight: We became "willing" to "agree with our adversaries," obey God's command to "love your neighbor as yourself;" and to set things right with others.

[Again, "willingness" came from John 7:17; "agreeing with your adversaries" came from the sermon on the mount, Matthew 5:25; obeying God's command to "love your neighbor," from 1 John 4:20, James 2:8, and elsewhere. Once again, the emphasis was on the need to "*do* the will of

God" in order to "know" the things that cannot be seen but are promised by God. See Clarence I. Benson, *The Eight Points of the Oxford Group* (London: Oxford University Press, 1936), p. 135. The key thought was that obedience is the organ of spiritual knowledge.]

Nine: We took action to (1) reconcile ourselves with any brother that had anything against us; (2) restore to him anything wrongfully taken from him; and (3) forgive him for any of his trespasses against us.

[Several A.A. Bible sources directly support this "restitution" idea which was so important in the Oxford Group. But its main Bible roots are in the sermon on the mount and were frequently quoted in early A.A. Thus, "reconciliation" is from Matthew 5:23. "Restoration," as part of that reconciliation, is primarily from the account about Zacchaeus in Luke 19:1-10. Forgiving trespasses is most forcefully contained in the verses from Matthew 6:12, 14-15, in the sermon.]

Ten: We *continued* to watch for, and pray for the removal of, those "major" sins blocking us from fellowship with God—namely resentment, selfishness, dishonesty, and fear. When they cropped up, we applied the same corrective steps involved in our initial housecleaning; we tried to adhere to a new code of love and tolerance; and we began reaching out to others.

[If you have learned the first nine steps, you have learned the A.A. formula for the life-change, of which the Oxford Group and Anne Smith wrote so frequently. Surrender, self-examination, confession, conviction, conversion, and then continuance were the codified Oxford Group and biblical ideas. Step Ten was *about* the continuance process, as were the last two steps. Anne Smith, Sam Shoemaker, and Oxford Group writers called the process "Conservation" and "Continuance." They also called it "daily surrender." A.A. mostly called it "spiritual growth." See Dick B., *The Oxford Group and Alcoholics Anonymous: A Design for Living*

That Works, 2d ed. (Kihei, HI: Paradise Research Publications, 1998), pp. 221-68. The most significant Bible root was Matthew 26:41—"Watch and pray, that ye enter not into temptation: the spirit *is* willing, but the flesh *is* weak." See Dick B., *The Good Book and The Big Book: A.A.'s Roots in the Bible*, 2d ed., 1997, pp. 160-62.]

Eleven: Before retiring, we checked our behavior against Christ's moral standards, asking forgiveness where we had failed to observe them and guidance toward doing better in the future. We sought daily fellowship with God and other believers through Bible study, prayer, seeking His guidance, reading Christian literature, and often through church attendance. We turned to God for peace, and our reliance on Him provided relief from anxiety and fear.

[The Eleventh Step starts at night—not in the morning. The evening inventory is to see and correct any failures to do the Tenth Step correctly. Then comes the "prayer and meditation." There are many biblical aspects of the Eleventh Step roots; and we give them in detail in *The Good Book and The Big Book*. You begin by asking God's forgiveness for failures (1 John 1:9). Next, with asking His guidance for all your steps (Proverbs 3:5-6). Then comes the morning. There are countless verses that support the so-called "morning watch" or "quiet time." The complete picture is explained in Dick B., *Good Morning! Quiet Time, Morning Watch, Meditation, and Early A.A.*, 2d ed. (Kihei, HI: Paradise Research Publications, 1998). Unfortunately, almost all the current discussions of "meditation" just plain delete the real basic requirement. Early A.A. and biblical Quiet Time begins with acceptance of Jesus Christ as Lord and Saviour (Romans 10:9). When the spirit of God has been received through the new birth, that spirit of God communicates with our promised gift of the Holy Spirit (1 Corinthians 12). After being sealed with this spirit of promise, we can and do receive communication from, and can communicate directly with God, utilizing the Bible, prayer, God's revelations, reading the informative Christian literature, and—in the Oxford Group—writing down thoughts and "checking" them against Scripture. Proper prayer, supplication, and renewal of the mind with God's truth assures a peace of God that "passes understanding." Dealing with, and overcoming anxiety, fear, and doubt is best covered in the sermon on the mount—Matthew 6:25-34 and Philippians 4:6-7). This does not mean "acceptance." As Dr. Bob pointed out, "First Things First" means "seek ye first the kingdom of God and his righteousness."]

Twelve: Having received the power of God through accepting Christ, and having the ability to bring into manifestation that power of the Holy Spirit, we passed on to others the steps we had taken, and tried to do God's will in all our affairs—particularly emphasizing the principles spelled out in 1 Corinthians 13.

[For receipt of the power of God through "conversion," see the correspondence between Bill Wilson and Dr. Carl Jung and *Pass It On* (New York: Alcoholics Anonymous World Services, Inc., 1984), pp. 381-86; Acts 1:8—"But ye shall receive power, after that the Holy Ghost is come upon you. . .;" and Acts 4:10—"Be it known unto you all, and to all the people of Israel, that by the name of Jesus Christ of Nazareth, whom ye crucified, whom God raised from the dead, *even* by him doth this man stand here before you whole" ("this man" is the man who was lame from birth and was healed by the Apostle Peter in the name of Jesus Christ—Acts 3:1-12). For witnessing, see 2 Corinthians 5:20—"ambassadors for Christ" and Acts 26:22—"Having therefore obtained help of God, I continue unto this day witnessing both to small and great, saying none other things than those which the prophets and Moses did say should come: That Christ should suffer, and that he should be the first that should rise from the dead, and should shew light unto the people, and to the Gentiles." Note that Bill Wilson's "sponsor" Ebby Thacher *did* receive help of God and then specifically said so to Wilson: "God has done for me what I could not do for myself"—a recurrent A.A. theme and phrase. For the principles of love to be practiced, see

Henry Drummond's *The Greatest Thing in the World* and 1 Corinthians 13. The principles *in their entirety* included all God's commandments. See Ecclesiastes 12:13: "Let us hear the conclusion of the whole matter; Fear [revere] God, and keep his commandments; for this *is* the whole *duty* of man."]

Shall You Cram *Your* Bible into Today's A.A.?

Lots of people have tried to cram the Bible into the Twelve Steps, presumably to convince Christians and perhaps AAs that the two can be reconciled. [See, for example, *Serenity: A Companion for Twelve Step Recovery* (Nashville: Thomas Nelson, 1990); and there are several other "Twelve-Step Bibles."] But I strongly believe there is no fruit in putting out such "Twelve-Step Bibles" for Christians to read or for AAs to read or for Christian AAs to read. First, because considerable research has not turned up voluminous Scripture behind the original thinking, study, and ideas AAs borrowed from the Bible. Second, because some of the "biblical" ideas AAs, the Oxford Group, and Shoemaker borrowed and used did not in fact rightly-divide God's Word.

I take the position that A.A. language is A.A. language, and that what is in the Bible is not *today* to be *privately* interpreted in light of the Twelve Steps, injected into the Twelve Steps, or used to teach the Twelve Steps. See 2 Peter 1:20—"Knowing this first, that no prophecy of the scripture is of any private interpretation." The Bible itself was written for believers. Nearly all the early AAs were believers. And they took, as Dr. Bob put it, "what they needed" primarily from three segments of the Bible—the sermon on the mount (Matthew 5-7); 1 Corinthians 13; and the Book of James. *These* segments can and *should* be compared today with and to A.A. ideas in order to see and understand what the early AAs were using and studying. [My most recent (and I believe, my best) effort at so doing is in Appendix 2 of Dick B., *Why Early A.A. Succeeded: The Good Book in Alcoholics Anonymous Yesterday and Today (A Bible Study Primer for AAs and other 12-Steppers)*. (Kihei, HI: Paradise Research Publications, 2001), pp. 225-65.].

But cramming *your* Bible into the Twelve Steps (be it Roman Catholic, Hebrew, or King James) or even into the Big Book text is unlikely to enlighten anyone—not believers, not unbelievers, and not

AAs, whether they are believers or not. Those well-intentioned Christians who try to fashion a new A.A. *in* the Bible itself do not seem to get the point of the following verse. A verse which I think is most relevant Scripture for those who insist on combining the Bible and the A.A. text *as if* they were related:

> Jesus answered and said unto them, Ye do err, not knowing the scriptures, nor the power of God (Matthew 22:29).

The Scriptures did not contain nor have anything to do with the Twelve Steps. And God's power hardly depends on His commanding or on your taking Twelve Steps, either at the time the Bible was written or now. Study or learning or knowledge of the Bible and the power of God is little enhanced by reading "Steps" or a "recovery" text written by someone like Bill Wilson, who knew little of the Bible, never joined a church, and never did much religious reading at all. Any connection between the Bible and today's A.A. is much diminished if not gone, thanks to the contemporary "immersing" and "universalizing" of A.A.'s program to make it acceptable to anyone at all, regardless of what they believe or whether they believe anything at all.

Most Pioneer AAs were not Bible students. Generally speaking, neither are today's AAs. At least not many today. In fact, most of us in A.A. who are Bible students run into all kinds of flack if and when we even mention the Bible. It is fair to say that the Bible itself was left on the podium at Akron Number One some time before Dr. Bob died, and was very much ignored thereafter.

On the other hand, *some important truths* in the Bible *were* studied, believed, and applied by the Pioneers. AAs *did* seek God. (See Matthew 6:33.) They did conclude that God *is*. (See Hebrews 11:6.) They did rely on God. (See Proverbs 3:5-6.)They did study some important biblical truths about God (Almighty, Creator, Maker, Father, Spirit, love, grace, mercy, power, and so on). They accepted certain important principles concerning God (love—1 John 4:8; prayer and meditation—Psalms 5:1-3; healing, forgiveness, and redemption—Psalm 103; studying His Word—2 Timothy 2:15; revelation in the Bible—2 Timothy 3:15-16; a new birth—John 3; revelation to born-again believers—1 Corinthians 2:7-11; and doing the will of God—Matthew 6:10). These truths were in the Good Book. They were available for study topically in *The Runner's Bible* and the daily devotionals like *The Upper Room*, that Pioneers read.

[See Dick B., *The Books Early AAs Read for Spiritual Growth*, 7th ed. (Kihei, HI: Paradise Research Publications, 1998)]. And so on.

But let it go at that! There is no point in multiplying Bible sizes by putting Twelve Step history, statements, principles, references and explanations on every other page! As examples of this problem see: (1) *Recovery Devotional Bible* (Grand Rapids, MI: Zondervan Publishing House, 1993); (2) *Serenity: A Companion for Twelve Step Recovery* (Nashville: Thomas Nelson, 1990); and (3) *The Life Recovery Bible* (Wheaton, IL: Tyndale House Publishers, 1992). In fact, before the "recovery" industry began to crash in the early 1990's, it would appear that several, major, religious publishing houses took a crack at trying to reconcile the Bible and the Twelve Steps.

But let it go! A.A. principles can be seen and studied by themselves. Some of these principles flatly ignore the Bible. Some are at variance with the Bible. Some were truly borrowed from the Bible. Some, rightly or wrongly, quote Scripture. But most A.A. principles should not be taught as if they were Scriptural. They are not. And they should not be written into Bibles on every other page in an attempt to force A.A. into the Bible or the Bible into A.A., while A.A. is in fact departing therefrom with great and determined haste these days. Or so it seems.

If you are a believer, you can take heart from the success *early* AAs had in relying on the Creator, studying about Him in the Bible, and trying to live by the principles laid down in the Bible. You can ignore those who say the Bible is irrelevant in A.A. or that you can believe anything you want to. Those statements may be true for some. But the "some" need not include you. Of course, you can subscribe to those views if you are foolish enough to believe that such ideas will cure you. Dr. Bob did not. Bill Dotson did not. And Bill Wilson did not for the first few years of his intense association with Dr. Bob and with Reverend Sam Shoemaker.

How Do You Help the Unbeliever?

You probably will not. Today, that is. You probably cannot. You may not want to. And you probably should not. But give the new guy a break. Let him breathe first—in and out!

As I said, the Bible was written for believers. It describes God's major sacrifice for, and major promise to, those who want to believe. (See John 3:16 and Romans 10:9, 10.) But it is the individual who has

What History Can Teach You in, and about, A.A. Itself 65

to decide what is true or false. It is the individual who has to decide whether the Bible is truth. It is the individual who has to decide whether *Yahweh* is, whether He loves and cares, and whether He will cure. It is the individual who has to decide whether Jesus Christ is the way, the truth, and the life. That is true in or out of A.A. You either decide that you want to come to God the same way the early Christians came—primarily as described in the Book of Acts. Or you decide not to. Early AAs decided to go the Christian way. They gave it their best shot. And when they did, they were cured in astonishing percentages. That was enough for those who were their immediate followers.

Today, things are different. Today, a newcomer marches in our doors. Maybe he was forced to come. Maybe he was reluctant to come. Maybe he decides he should not have come. Maybe he does not like what he sees. Maybe he does not want to quit drinking. Maybe he thinks he has no drinking problem. Maybe he thinks he has a drinking problem, but it is someone else's fault. Maybe he just wants friends who understand him. Maybe he is just checking things out. Maybe he is a Christian, and maybe he is not. Maybe he is angry with God. Maybe he is angry with his church. Maybe he is angry "with the nuns." Maybe he is just plain angry. Maybe he is a rebel—someone who tells you he does not like what you believe even though he has no well-defined belief himself. Maybe he cannot identify with the crowd. Maybe he just wants to get the heat off, or go on the wagon, or put on a show for someone. Maybe—and all too often—he just wants to turn tail and get the heck out of the room. And find the quickest route to the bar.

Then he hears that his "higher power can be a radiator." If I had heard that, I'd have lit out of the place right then and there. Yet people keep telling that stuff—"he" or "she" or "it" [that "higher power"] can be a radiator, a chair, a lightbulb, Santa Claus, a table, someone, something, self, a group, or nothing at all. But are there are newcomers stupid enough to believe it?

Only after they have had it pounded into their heads by people at meetings, counselors, history books, and outsiders that A.A. is not religious, but spiritual. Only after they repeatedly hear that you can believe anything you want to. Or that you can believe that *your* "higher power" can be a "door knob" or just about anything "greater than yourself." People must believe it, or pretend to believe it, because AAs and others say it or write it quite frequently these days.

And what a pity! What a repudiation of all that the A.A. pioneers believed, developed, and tried to pass along.

Maybe the newcomer hears the word "God." Maybe he hears the word "Bible." These days he will probably never hear the words "Jesus Christ" or "Holy Spirit." He will hear many say that they were or are Roman Catholics; and no one says a word in protest. But let some unwary Protestant mention his Baptist church or Jesus as the Way or that he read the Bible before he came to the meeting; and the newcomer will probably hear someone screaming that the Twelve Traditions are being violated. The screamers never say what Traditions are allegedly being violated, or how they are being violated. But they sure make the claim. And in stentorian tones that would intimidate anyone but a Tenth Century Crusader.

What do you do with the newcomer under any of the foregoing circumstances? As I said, I try to get to know them and make them feel welcome. I offer to help. Then I eventually give them the five words (terms)—"God, Jesus Christ, Holy Spirit, the Bible" or "the door." And if they truly want to seek help from someone else, that is their privilege. If they are an atheist, I may point them to an atheist; but my witnessing is over. I am firm on that today. I just do not think that present-day A.A. is so situated that I should try to "return it to Christianity," convert unwilling people to Christ, or fight out the battle of faith in a room full of people who want to fight or have just never equated God with recovery. And probably will not. My view is that the place to make the decision about the newcomer is not in the meeting. It is in the personal conversation where he is at ease, the discussion is private, and the choice is made by him without intimidation or misinformation.

I tell anyone in A.A. our history if they want to know it. And I think all deserve to know it because it is so relevant to the successful program early AAs developed. But it is not the program of today. And, if no one wants to believe what people used to believe and used to do, then so be it. Dr. Bob said in his personal story that he felt sorry for such people. Bill Wilson wrote in the Big Book: God either is, or He isn't. And if that does not do it for the unbeliever, probably nothing will—at least not until they go through the revolving doors enough times to be willing to try something "different." Something that worked quite well over sixty years ago.

How Can You Help a Believer in, or into, A.A.?

A host of people do not even try any longer. There is no towering, stern, well-educated, Christian physician like our co-founder Dr. Robert Holbrook Smith—who had been cured himself—to lay it out cold for them. Therefore, the question is whether or not to surrender to the amorphous mass of new theories and chatter pouring through the rooms, or to really endeavor to help the new believers in or into the rooms if that is what they want to do. That *is* what I wanted when I came into the rooms. I wanted help—just like the help I have wanted when I went to the doctor, the clergyman, and the nurse. I was exposed to the amorphous mass by total strangers. And—for the most part—I had to deal with it alone amongst a host of people who were not even close to being believers. Since then, however, I have since encountered thousands who are believers, who are bewildered, and who want help and guidance as believers. Help and guidance from you and from me, and certainly help and guidance from *Yahweh* their God—the Creator of Whom the Big Book speaks so many times.

You can help them by telling them the obvious—the truth!

- There is no requirement for membership in A.A. today. In fact, there are no members!

- There are all kinds in A.A. Some are sick. Some are well. Some think they are well. Some are angry. Some are nice. Some are both. Some are helpful. Some are selfish. Some are both. Some have studied the Big Book and "taken the Twelve Steps." Some have not. In fact, most have not. Some are fit to be sponsors, as A.A. sees sponsorship today. Some are not. Most do not know the difference. Some believe. Some do not. Most do not have any convictions at all, about religion, about belief, or about God. And on and on. The truth to tell is about the diversity in A.A.'s newcomer, old-timer, and revolving door population.

- There are no "official" leaders or teachers any more. Dr. Bob died in 1950, 15 years after A.A. began. His wife Anne died shortly before him in 1949. Bill Wilson died in 1971, more than 30 years ago. And the Twelve Traditions merely say that "our leaders" today are just trusted servants who do not govern and proclaim that the ultimate authority is a loving God as He may express Himself in a group conscience—not as He may express Himself in the Bible, or by direct revelation, or to believers. No! Just to any assembled group—believers and unbelievers alike.

- If you are looking for "the" recovery program, it is not in the meetings. It is not in the conferences or roundups or conventions or bashes. Not in the dances. Not in the assemblies. Not in the literature. Not in the words of your sponsor or someone else's sponsor. Not in the words of your therapist or treatment center or the recovery literature that abounds. Today, that recovery program is in the Doctor's Opinion and the first 164 pages of the latest edition of *Alcoholics Anonymous*. That "basic text" is in its Fourth Edition. The stories of the Pioneers have, for the most part, been removed. The stories of today bear little resemblance to the stories told by the pioneers of Akron City Hospital between 1935 and 1938.

- If you are going to be a Boy Scout, study the Boy Scout Manual. I did! If you are going to be a soldier, study the Army Field Manuals. I did. If you are going to go to "Cal," study the textbooks the professor assigns. I did. If you are going to go to Stanford Law School, study the case books, the professor assigns. I did. There is lots more to be said in these realms. But I hope the point is made. If you are going to be an AA, study *the* Alcoholics Anonymous text book and take the Steps in accordance with the Big Book directions!

- But who is going to explain the Big Book and tell you how to take the Steps? You'd be amazed at how few people are able to do that. The Big Book is well written. It is brief. It states it was written to provide specific directions. But, for the sick newcomer, it is about as easy to read and understand as an Algebra or Trigonometry textbook when you first see it. But today, there are some fine people who have prepared some excellent seminars and guides to the Steps and Big Book. Several have devoted years to studying and teaching these subjects. They are AAs. They are gnarled veterans. And they serve without pay!

- But you need to remember that you are a believer. You are trying to help a believer, whether that believer is yourself or not. So the rest of this commentary is for you!

- Stand on the proposition that the Word of God contains truth (John 17:17: "Sanctify them through thy truth: thy word is truth").

- Stand on the proposition that God wants all men to be saved and come unto the knowledge of the truth (1 Timothy 2:3-4: "For this is good and acceptable in the sight of God our Saviour; Who will have all men to be saved, and to come unto the knowledge of the truth").

- Stand on the proposition that you are saved by doing what Romans 10:9 prescribes: "That if thou shalt confess with thy mouth the Lord Jesus, and shalt believe in thine heart that God hath raised him from the dead, thou shalt be saved").

- From that point on, stand on the proposition that you have as much right to attend A.A. or any Twelve Step group as anyone else. If someone tells you what you can or cannot say or what you can or cannot do or what you can or cannot believe or what you should or should not believe, that person is wrong!

- You can believe in God and say so. You can believe that Jesus Christ is the Way and say so. You can study the Bible and say so. You can believe in the gift of the Holy Spirit and say so. *What you believe is none of A.A.'s business.* That you believe these things just happens to be totally consistent with what the A.A. founders believed. And you need to learn that and know that and say so. Furthermore, A.A.'s own "Conference Approved" literature supports all these views. But that literature is getting harder and harder to find. It is seldom discussed. And the A.A. leaders of today are litigators and have the money to litigate. They do litigate, and their actions do intimidate even though A.A.'s Tenth Tradition suggests: ". . . [T]he A.A. name ought never be drawn into public controversy."

- Stand on the proposition that the A.A. program of today specifically declares: "Love and tolerance of others is our code" (*Alcoholics Anonymous*, 4th ed., p. 84).

- If some "leader" or someone attending a meeting violates that tolerance code, you do not have to take a swing at him or battle with him. Ask God what to do. Ask God in the name of Jesus Christ. Silently label the intolerant person wrong and "intolerant." Don't buy what he says. He is the one who is intolerant and uniformed. Ignore him and, if he becomes intimidating or obnoxious, vote with your feet. Leave! In the county where I got sober in California, there were over 300 meetings each week. There is plenty of room in the rooms for you; and there are plenty of really great people who will love you, help you, inform you, and help you to help others. That is the program at its best, and it still exists in full force! Leave the angry ones alone. They do not want help. They do not want you. And they do not want knowledge. They just want to blow. I used to tell my sponsees the story of the "whirling dervishes." They were the intruders who intimidated Camel Caravans by shouting, waving knives, and flashing black robes. What do you do with the whirling dervishes in a "self-help" meeting? Let 'em whirl. Just get out of their way.

- Get hooked up with God as quickly as possible. This may mean reading the Bible often. It may mean reading books about the Bible often. It may mean praying often. It may mean learning to pray the way Jesus taught people to pray. It may mean keeping your reading, your thinking, your speaking, and your actions focused on God's ways, not man's ways. It may mean learning quickly the difference between what people say and what God's says. It may mean recognizing the fiery darts of the devil when they come flying your way and sending them elsewhere. It certainly may mean seeking the help of religious teachers, clergy, and religious materials. It may mean attending church or a Bible fellowship. It may mean seeking and keeping company with believers—in and out of A.A.

Do You Alter the Text and Steps to Suit Your Beliefs?

The Boy Scouts, the Army, the University of California, and Stanford Law School may not always have believed or taught what I wanted to hear. But I did not make it my mission to change these outfits. I was there for a reason. And it was incumbent upon me to stick by their rules—not necessarily to believe them. For the most part, of course, I did. They were good rules.

I did not come to A.A. to alter any rules. I was far too sick to know the rules, learn the rules, or even follow the rules. So I did what I was told as far as the unwritten rules were concerned: Go to meetings. Get a sponsor. Study the Big Book. Take the Steps. Get a commitment as a greeter or a coffee maker or a setup person. Go to the meetings early and leave late. Get telephone numbers, and use them. Hang out with the "winners"—whoever they were! Stay away from slippery places and slippery people. Don't drink, no matter what. But none of those things helped me overcome fear, guilt, shame, anxiety, loneliness, confusion, forgetfulness, and so many of other negatives that arise out of a depressed, brain damaged, ineffective, "screwed up" thought process and way of living. There had to be change.

What about the Twelve Steps? I reviewed the Steps in a historical perspective. But I did not and do not advocate changing the Steps themselves because you cannot change the rules without changing the program. If everybody put words like Buddha, Jesus, Group, Something, or Self in the Steps in place of God, you wouldn't have the original program. Nor would you have the present program. Nor are you likely to have a program based on 65 years of experience with drunks and with drunks helping drunks.

So what do *you* do with the Twelve Steps? Learn them and take them is my suggestion. Of course, you also have the option to ignore them and get another program. That is also my suggestion if that is how you, as a believer, feel about them. But do not try to mix the Steps and their language with some ideas of another program or your own self-made program.

How a Believer Might *View* the Steps, and *Not Edit* Them

About the First Step

The First Step in A.A. basically has you admit you should not drink and that your life is messed up. That is a sane proposition. The difficulty is that it uses the word "powerless." And that word has given rise to endless hunks of baloney. People frequently say: "I'm powerless over people, places, and things." Says who! Not the Steps or the Big Book. Or they just emphasize that they are "powerless" over alcohol. Says who! If that were really so, there is no way out for you or for me; and that is a dilemma in the purported logic that some of us see. So we just point out that the rest of the Steps are about "finding" God and the power of God. So the program does offer a way out. The pioneers even considered using that name—"the way out." I think "powerless" is a lousy word and that Bill's own language in his Big Book story is far better: Alcohol was my master, he said—thus "taking" the First Step. Later, he wrote that he was "licked." I buy either one, and I can understand either idea. Why? Because I had become subservient to alcohol. My life stunk. I was getting whipped in every battle in which I was engaged. God hears and honors the plea: "God help me." He does not need to have you say "I'm powerless." See Psalm 34:6, "This poor man cried, and the Lord heard him, and saved *him* out of all his troubles."

About the Second Step

The Second Step did not exist in the early program. Furthermore, the earlier drafts of the Steps assumed the existence of God and that He could and would restore you to sanity. In essence, the real basic is that you need to, and can come to: (1) believe in God; (2) believe he can restore you to sane thinking (rejecting the booze that is destroying you), and (3) understand that sanity is simply your ability to see and avoid the "cunning, baffling, and powerful" foes—excessive drinking, and the inevitable dire consequences that result from it. Any other aspect of the Second Step, as Bill revised it, is simply not helpful to me and flouts the Bible teachings about salvation and how to come to God. So I just tell the sponsee: There are *two* words for you in the Second Step—God and Sanity. Believe in the first.

What History Can Teach You in, and about, A.A. Itself 73

Understand what the second means. See 2 Timothy 1:7: "For God hath not given us the spirit of fear; but of power, and of love, and of a sound mind."

About the Third Step

The Third Step was intended to cover the idea of "surrender." But Bill got that concept thoroughly mixed up with the "self-surrender" teachings of Professor William James and Reverend Sam Shoemaker. This, in turn, has people "giving their will to God"—something they cannot do—and then "taking their will back"—also something they cannot do. God tells us how to "surrender" and become His kids. See John 3—"ye must be born again"—born of the spirit of God. Then see Romans 10:9—which tells you how to do it: confess that Jesus is Lord and believe that God raised him from the dead. This really causes the rest of Bill's Third Step thinking to be primarily a William James-Sam Shoemaker route to God that was not part of Akron A.A., nor of the Bible, nor of Christian belief. On the other hand, Bill does suggest some ideas that can be useful to know and are necessary to an understanding of the rest of his Steps: (1) That self-propulsion—trying to run the world to suit yourself—is doomed to fail. (2) That such an approach is labeled self-centeredness and ego-centricity. (3) That the first move in abandoning the behavior is making a decision to quit playing God. (4) That the next one is to believe and understand that God *is* God. (5) Finally that you pray for Him to guide you to do His will, not yours if it conflicts. Is that useful? I have found it so. And it assists in understanding the next few steps.

About Steps Four, Five, and Six

The Fourth, Fifth, and Sixth Steps are kind of a mish-mash of religious ideas. [See, for example, the comments of a Christian writer, Tim Stafford, in "The Hidden Gospel of the 12 Steps," *Christianity Today*, July 22, 1991. Compare the conclusion by Dr. Randolph Atkins that A.A. *is* a religion (Randolph Gilbert Atkins, Jr., *"No Outside Enterprises:" Rational Recovery's Countermovement Challenge to the Institutionalization of the Twelve-Step Movement in American Addiction Care.* Ph.D. Dissertation, University of Virginia, January, 2000.) And note the severe lashing A.A. received in Martin and Deidre Bobgan's *12 Steps to Destruction: Codependency Recovery Heresies* (Santa Barbara, CA: EastGate Publishers, 1991).]

As to the Fourth Step, there is, in the sermon on the mount, what might be labeled a call for looking for the mote or beam in your own eye and casting it out—before you start working on the next guy's speck in the eye. But neither the sermon on the mount nor the Bible itself singles out resentment, self-centeredness, dishonesty, and fear as *the* beams to be located or to be the sole basis for specifying the areas for amends. Bill did nonetheless did just that in the Fourth Step. Then, ignoring the "purity" absolute; he mixed in sex and departed from what the Bible teaches about sex. And it teaches plenty! When I look at the Fourth Step, I see that resentment, self-centeredness, dishonesty, and fear are not only condemned in the Bible (but not necessarily in those words); they are also examples of techniques involved in "playing God"—yet doing it in ways that do not work and cause misery. That can be useful information. Trying to run the world yourself *does* engender resentment when people do not march to your tune. Claiming to be the CEO/runner of the world (an ego-centric) is just plain nonsense and destined to produce conflict. Dishonesty often involves a "secret" realization that your rules do not work while God's rules do. And fear may be the result of believing or learning you cannot run the world and yet are without the power to fend off the consequences—lacking a reliance on the Creator, His commandments, and His power. Is that information useful? Assuming I am correct in my interpretation of Bill's writing, it can be. But it omits a zillion other faults and sins. Moreover, when Bill's Jesuit advisers edited his Twelve and Twelve, they apparently persuaded him there were at least "seven deadly sins," instead of the four he had previously specified. Finally, pioneers like Clarence Snyder dug up an inventory that looks more a catalog of all the sins specified in the church epistles instead of the "four" or "seven" Bill Wilson, his editors, or the pioneers themselves chose to identify.

As to the Fifth Step, the Bible commands that you confess your sins to God and then receive His forgiveness (1 John 1:9). It also suggests that you confess your faults one to another so that others can pray for you and you can be healed (James 5:16). The two verses are not inconsistent, but the Fifth Step is generally assumed to be based on James 5:16. The Big Book embellishes the process, proclaiming you should "confess" to God, to yourself, and to another human being. This language has caused problems for Roman Catholics;

problems in dealing with 1 John 1:9, and problems of *private* biblical interpretation that Bill inherited from Oxford Group language.

As to the Sixth Step, I'd just point to its recognition of the need to abandon the sins and change. I'd also say its recognizes the importance of God's help. Both ideas are useful But the further idea that, in the Sixth Step process, your are expecting God to eliminate sinning from your life leaves many with the idea that they will not sin once they have completed the Seventh Step. Such reasoning, if correct, would eliminate need for the rest of the Steps, flout the teachings of the Bible, and certainly ignore our "old man" nature which leaves us free to pursue sinful conduct any time we choose.

About the Seventh Step

I find Step Seven quite difficult to explain or understand. It suggests that God *eliminates* your sinning, that humility is about the only requirement for His help, and that a prayer will do the job. If it originally involved the need for "conversion" (and it originally did), I have a problem with the fact that it does not say so. Bill W. said so to Dr. Carl Jung. If it conveys the idea that man will never again sin, it is absurd. For it fails to acknowledge that Jesus Christ made available *remission of sins past* and intercedes for the believer as to *forgiveness of future sins.* It thus presents serious biblical problems. It should therefore be handled as just another of Bill's self-constructed religious ideas, and then allowed to lie—except for the concept that there will be no overcoming of any sins—past or present—without believing on Jesus Christ.

About the Eighth Step

The Eighth Step can best be understood as saying that one should list the wrongs and required amends he discovered from the Fourth Step and then become willing to make them. I do not have a problem with this idea.

About the Ninth Step

The Ninth Step calls for action to right the wrongs. Its basic ideas come from the Bible. And, as long as one does not expect heavenly forgiveness or eternal salvation to result from his restitutions, I do not have a problem with that one either. However, because it lacks the simple idea of the Oxford Group (*"not who's* right, but *what's* right") it has produced lots of theological nonsense. Today, many AAs write letters of apology to dead relatives. Some do penance by setting aside money for charity or newcomers. Some merely feel guilty for years and years, whether they make their amends or not. None of this is biblical; it ignores what God makes available to believers, and it is not even sound thinking ("For by grace are ye saved through faith; and that not of yourselves: *it is* the gift of God. Not of works, lest any man should boast"—Ephesians 2:8-9).

About the Tenth Step

The Tenth Step calls for an AA to be on the alert. If his sins, faults, and misdeeds appear on the scene again, he has to do something about them *immediately*. And the formula for rectification comes from the previous steps. I have no problem with continuing vigilance. The Bible tells us to be sober and vigilant and resist the devil's overtures (1 Peter 5:8-9). Sam Shoemaker commented that the devil always comes back along familiar paths. I like both of those concepts. We need to be watchful; and we need to assume that the devil will attack our weakest flank—the addiction or weakness that caused the most trouble and brought the most temporary joy (See James 1:12-16). You can consider these ideas and use them in conjunction with the Steps.

About the Eleventh Step

The Eleventh Step is just plain over Bill Wilson's head. Bill's prayer and meditation thoughts are worthy. But his application of them is not biblical. The Eleventh Step calls for prayer. That's good. It also calls for "meditation," and that has been grossly misunderstood and has been confusing. It calls for reviewing conduct at the end of the day, asking forgiveness where there was failure, and seeking God's guidance for corrective behavior. Not bad at all. It calls for morning communication with God. But it leaves out the need to be born again, the need to study the Bible, the need to pray as God directs, and the believer's holy spirit to which God can and does speak. Bill's other comments go astray on a merry path of "intuition," "inspiration," "practice," and other thoughts derived in part from the Oxford Group, in part from the mystics, in part from "mind science," and in part from "New Thought" writings. The Bible is left to one side. Then Bill urges his readers to be quick to see where religious people are right and to make use of what they have to offer. Not bad as an idea and one which Bill should have followed, but seldom acceptable to the AAs who do the most talking at meetings. They do not like to talk about rabbis and ministers; yet we do often hear priests and nuns speak. They do not like mention of the Bible. Some condemn use of some of religious literature such as Emmet Fox's *The Sermon on the Mount* that was used in early A.A. This mess can be summed up by saying you cannot be all things to all people and still claim to be walking God's ways as they are prescribed in the Bible. Not when you introduce polyglot and self-made religion. The last part of the Step suggests looking to God where there is indecision or anxiety. Good biblical thinking, but Bill's prescription for how to do it is not.

About the Twelfth Step

The Twelfth Step leads the believer astray. Biblically, there is no "spiritual awakening." There can be a new birth from above. There can be the receipt of the power of the Holy Spirit. There can be healing, forgiveness, and deliverance by God. But it does not involve some mystical "awareness" or "consciousness" or "personality change" which Bill interjected in Appendix Two when he eliminated "spiritual experience"—an Oxford Group phrase—and substituted "spiritual awakening," which also is an Oxford Group phrase. Furthermore, the Big Book's Appendix Two fails adequately to define an "awakening." That word was substituted for "experience"—the spiritual experience which Bill Wilson claimed to have had, but which was simply not the common platter of ordinary AAs. The expression came from the Oxford Group and partly from the universalized "religious experience" ideas of Professor William James. But there is no biblical basis for such ideas. The receipt of the gift of the Holy Spirit can be understood if one reads the Book of Acts and the Church Epistles. It can not be understood by reading the Big Book or by experiencing some mysterious "awakening"—either sudden or "educational," as so many like to phrase it. Next, if you cannot agree on what a religious or spiritual experience is, or on what a spiritual awakening is, you cannot pass on much of Bill's message. Bill's sponsor Ebby Thacher made it easy: "God has done for me what I could not do for myself." Ebby told that to Bill. I find that useful and often say so in my talks and discussions.

The final Twelfth Step idea ("practice these principles") falls into the pit because Bill did not seem to want to mention the principles. They probably were originally the Four Absolutes which Wilson did not like. They could have been the nine ingredients of love in 1 Corinthians 13, which Bill never seems to have mentioned. They could have included all the teachings of Christ. They could have included the Ten Commandments (and did in some early A.A. writing). Or they could simply have amounted to this: Learn all God's commandments, and obey them! But Wilson did not make clear what "these principles" were, so his audience is left to wonder.

Just How, Then, Can You Help a Believer

How, then, can you help a believer? To answer that question, you must deal with another question: If you want to help a believer, what do you do with the Steps. My answer? Read them. Make sure the believer has truly accepted Christ. Then caution him not to waste his time trying to reconcile the Steps with the Bible. Help him see that the Big Book is *not* the Bible. Confirm his understanding that the Word of God *is* the standard for God's truth. Help him realize that the Big Book itself is probably the only remaining standard in today's confused writings and talks that still stands for what the A.A. program of recovery really is. Then urge him to plunge ahead in "taking" the Steps and—most certainly—coming to a knowledge of the *truth in the Bible.* No matter what he hears. That is just what early AAs did with the Good Book.

Burn into your mind the plain statement by Dr. Robert Holbrook Smith, the co-founder of Alcoholics Anonymous, that the program's basic ideas came from the Bible. From the beginning of the program to the end of his life, Dr. Bob repeatedly urged and emphasized Bible study. Those facts being so, the Good Book is as much a part of the A.A. program as the fellowship, the Slogans, the Big Book, the Twelve Steps, the Twelve Traditions, and all the other literature that graces the literature tables in today's meetings.

Way back in its August-September, 1978 issue of *Box 4-5-9* (Volume 23, No. 4), A.A.'s own General Service Office wrote an article titled "What 'Conference-Approved' Means." A.A.'s General Service Office said:

What History Can Teach You in, and about, A.A. Itself 79

It does *not* mean the Conference disapproves of any other publications. Many local A.A. central offices publish their own meeting lists. A.A. as a whole does *not* oppose these, any more than A.A. disapproves of the Bible or any other publications from any source that A.A.'s find useful. What any A.A. member reads is no business of G.S.O., or of the Conference, naturally.

That paragraph and explanation from A.A. "management" itself is a forgotten classic. It should be reprinted in A.A. literature often, regularly, and widely. And quoted frequently!

5
Offering More Than Abstinence

There is a big gap within the various Twelve Step Fellowships in the principles, care, and cure of the alcoholic or addict that a particular fellowship offers. Why? In large part this is the case because all have forgotten where they came from. Some of the missing elements can and should be supplied by knowledgeable members themselves. Some can be the subject of your help. Some require lots of outside help.

Many, if not most, newcomers enter the rooms and flounder about—detoxing, shaky, bewildered, fear-filled, guilt-ridden, ashamed, malnourished, penniless, jobless, with pains in their teeth, with broken bones and bandages, lonely, and (both biblically and in fact) without Christ, having no hope, and without God in the world (see Ephesians 2:12). They can either be left in that condition and told to quit drinking; or they can get the idea right away that there is more to sobriety, recovery, and cure than just quitting drinking and using. In fact, if the new person is not pointed to better ways in early sobriety, he is likely to remember best, and seek the solace of, his long-standing friends of the past (alcohol and drugs). You may not be a physician or a clergyman; but, as Bill Wilson put it, you can regard them as the experts and yourself as their "assistants."

Filling the Glass to "Full"

Most of us have heard the old saw: Either you see the glass as half empty or you see it as half full. And that may be OK when you are thankless, despairing, and just beginning. But I did not want to be "half-healed," or "half-recovered," or "half-well." Would you! We need to be shooting for the moon or we may never leave the launching pad. There is so much more that needs to be offered to the person who wants to get well, be cured, get on with a quality life, and serve God. Here are some of the practical needs that go far beyond early sobriety.

First, on the Medical Side

There are many risks not appreciated by the newcomer at all and often not understood by members or outsiders.

Suicide and suicidal talk. Thoughts of suicide are not an unusual item in early sobriety and abstinence. Both should be taken seriously. The newcomer enters because of a drinking or addiction problem. But other factors are often at work—life threats from others, major fear and guilt and shame ideas; severe depression from alcohol or drugs or biogenetic causes; legal and employment and marital problems; death in the family; bipolar maladies; criminal or bankruptcy proceedings; possible arrest; and a host of others. You see all the problems, but you may not see the possible results such as producing suicide. There is no attempt here to suggest medical diagnosis, prognosis, or treatment. But there are psychiatrists, psychologists, community mental health facilities, hotlines, and other sources that can be contacted. The newcomer needs help. He does not often recognize the problem. And you can be alert for the problem.

Detoxification shakes and sweats, seizures, and serious medical problems. Detox-related, medical problems are common and can be very serious. Old time AAs were usually hospitalized at the beginning. Some were in the hands of Dr. Bob. Some turned up at Towns Hospital in New York. And some were given old-fashioned A.A. first aid in the form of a "hummer" or a drink. Today's AAs know very little about spotting or solving these problems. The alcoholic who is starting to detox is often ignored in a meeting. I was in the process of having grand mal seizures, while my first sponsor was telling passers-by that I needed a meeting. Fortunately, an ambulance was called; and my life was saved by the para-medics, the emergency room physicians, and the staff at ICU. People with distended livers, damage from recent accidents, bleeding, broken bones, and other medical emergencies need help. Treatment centers and rehabs often refuse to admit someone who has not "detoxed" elsewhere. But where? The problems will seldom be dealt with soon

Offering More Than Abstinence

enough in A.A. You can be alert for the problem and seek professional aid.

Depressions of many varieties. Various kinds of depression are common. Too often, A. A. newcomers are told not to take pills. Too often, they are told they are "depressed" only because they have been taking depressants in the form of alcohol and drugs. Sometimes this is true; but there are also bipolar episodes that need medical treatment and perhaps drugs like lithium. There may be severe biogenetic depressions that can be treated with drugs like Zoloft. You can be alert for the depression problem and not slough off attention by feeling it is the alcoholic's fault or that it is something that is common and does not need treatment.

Second, on the Religious Side

It has become so common in fellowships today to ridicule or criticize or just plain out-short talk of religion, church, God, Jesus Christ, or the Bible that help of a religious nature may never come or be sought. This is just the opposite of the situation in Pioneer AA.

In early A.A., God came first. "First Things First" meant seeking God first. The Bible was the first book allowed the alcoholic for reading. Prayer was continuous—before, during, and after meetings, in the homes, and in fellowships. Religious literature, including the Bible, was the regular subject of study and discussion. You can return this resource to the alcoholic or addict, whether in or out of a Twelve Step group. There is ample history to support you. There are ample references to God, to helpful religious books, and to seeking the help of clergy even in today's Big Book. These also will support you. Furthermore, who cares! You do not have to let some ignorant dinosaur or some flamboyant newcomer intimidate you from believing in God and believing Dr. Bob's statement, "Your Heavenly Father will never let you down." Give a knockout blow to those who seek to destroy A.A.'s connection with the Creator.

Third, on the Economic Side

If you think most people come to A.A. at the top of the economic and social ladder, just listen to them.

Newcomers are often broke. They're often heavily in debt. They're often dodging creditors. They're often in trouble with taxes.

They frequently are uninsured and unlicenced drivers, uninsured against possible health problems, and uninsured as to other disasters. They may be overdue in alimony or child support payments. They may be unemployed or homeless or recently fired. They may be without any public or private assistance—unemployment, workmen's comp, disability, social security, pension, welfare, or general relief. They may be at the point of despair and disregard for all these problems; yet they will, sooner or later, face them and their consequences at every turn. The problems and their consequences can cause suicide, depression, drinking, drugging, violence, crime, homelessness, and many other social problems. You can recognize the problems and help the newcomer deal with them without become a lender, banker, or enabler. One of the first things I do is to check with the newcomer to see if he has "wants or warrants," "failures to appear," pending court dates, or outstanding criminal matters. The newcomer needs help. There are resources available. And you can help him acquire integrity, responsibility, accountability, and financial adequacy. Anne Smith pointed to God's will, as stated in 3 John 2, that He wished above all things that His kids prosper and be in health. [See Dick B., *Anne Smith's Journal, 1933-1939*, 3rd ed. (Paradise Research Publications, 1998), pp. 71, 133.] It is part of a new life in God's hands.

Fourth, on the Moral Side

Just go to an A.A., N.A., or other meeting and listen to the filthy language. Listen to the bragging about moral irresponsibility—as to unpaid taxes, mountainous debts, infidelity, revoked licenses, embezzled employers, under-the-table transactions, and all the rest. See how many in today's groups regard meetings as "meat markets" where an "easy lay" is the primary purpose and where "relationships" are the boasted achievements of so many.

These behaviors were not acceptable in early A.A. (except in the case of Bill Wilson, it seems). The Four Absolutes were the moral standards in A.A.. Responsibility, reconciliation, and restitution were part of the program. Adultery, fornication, and biblical sins were eschewed. Many might say that moral irresponsibility is the hallmark of America of today. But, within and without A.A., you can pull up the moral foundations of our churches, our schools, our government, our religions, and the Bible. You do not have to trumpet your views

Offering More Than Abstinence 85

in or out of meetings. But you can mightily proclaim the biblical history and precepts of early A.A. to your own protege and help him to stand!

Fifth, on the Fitness Side

Here's a real winning arena. Today's body builders, health and fitness fans, gyms, nutrition magazines, muscle magazines, and sports activities invite the alcoholic to return to health.

The average alcoholic suffers from malnutrition, physical deterioration, poor eating habits, poor exercise habits, ignored dental care, and poor hygiene. In today's society, restoration and improvement are watchwords. They offer good recovery, good health, good fitness, and high self-esteem as well as relief from depression, loneliness, and poor health. These can be stressed in and out of A.A. You can be one of those who stresses them, who encourages such activity, and who applauds each and every success—however great or small.

Sixth, on the Education Side

Devotion to alcohol, drugs, and the crimes that often go with them does not produce erudition. Early dropouts, lack of diplomas, substandard education, truancy, illiteracy, poor language, miserable writing, lack of comprehension, and lack of appropriate training and schooling and education are part and parcel of the alcohol scene.

Some newcomers cannot read. Some cannot write. Some cannot speak well. Some cannot comprehend well. And some come to meetings either embarrassed about, or hopelessly ignorant of, their educational shortcomings. Their return to drinking and drugging can actually be fostered by such mental inadequacies. And you can do something about that. You can spot the problems. You can compassionately approach their solution. You can locate resources. You can encourage seeking them. And you can applaud each and every success.

Seventh, on the Vocational and Employment Side

Many alcoholics and addicts still have retained adequate mental capacity—even after working for years at producing brain damage.

Their substance abuses, distorted ethics, missed days, lack of vocational training, and irresponsibility make them poor choices for employment. Many do not know this or care. But they are the derelicts of the future, and likely to be dead, jailed, or drunken bums if not armed with vocational skills.

Finally, There Are Special Needs within A.A. and Twelve Step Fellowships

Dr. Bob's wife Anne Ripley Smith was renowned for her work with newcomers and their families. Her journal is replete with practical suggestions for overcoming the problems mentioned above. She was characterized not only as a founder of A.A., but also as the "Mother of A.A." Friends wrote of her teaching, counseling, and Bible reading. They said she acted as nurse, evangelist, housekeeper, job adviser, and family counselor. She was a loyal and faith-filled wife. She was highly educated. She had been a teacher. She was knowledgeable of the Bible and of the Oxford Group. And she was compassionate, friendly, and understanding. Early AAs needed all her talents and more. And they received them frequently. The alcoholic who comes to A.A. today—merely abstaining from drinking, and confining himself to attending meetings—makes an unlikely prospect for those who count noses among the successful members. He who is mentally sick; he who is physically sick, malnourished, and out of shape; he who has no understanding of or relationship with God; he who has no job, no self-esteem, no education, no employment training or prospects, and no moral principles presents a sorry prospect for abstinence, recovery, sobriety, cure, and a successful life. And he often will get little help from his like-minded brothers and sisters who are simply rim-running meeting attenders.

You can help by example. You can help by what you say and share. You can help by what you do as a sponsor. You can help as an A.A. speaker. You can help as a physician, clergyman, counselor, therapist, government employee, non-profit social worker, health-care specialist, probation officer, correction officer, judge, parent, wife, sibling, or friend. If you understand the whole problem, you'll applaud the statement that "drinking's not the problem" and that "there's more to quitting drinking than quitting drinking."

Offering More Than Abstinence

Again, within and without A.A., You Can Help

As with all the other issues, there are plenty of resources. Just a lack of people who understand the needs, know the resources, and are willing to take a hands-on interest in helping the alcoholic/addict within the fellowships themselves. Yesterday I met one at the beach who was just out of prison, on parole, penniless, jobless, homeless, and virtually friendless. Yet he thought the solution to his problems was a return to meetings! You do not need to pass a sinking ship along to some other disaster-filled flotilla. You can be one of those who paddles a lifeboat and knows what it is supposed to do and where it is supposed to go.

And Help Is on the Way

In more and more areas of our country, there is heightened interest in communities, camps, and houses for troubled youths. And many of these young people do have trouble with alcohol and drugs. In the new "programs," they are not simply given Twelve Steps and told to go to meetings. They are given discipline. They are given training in working with others. They are given health, fitness, and nutrition information. They are given exposure to vocational training. They are given education. They are given friendship and encouragement. Some in Florida and elsewhere are given some solid grounding in the Bible and trust in God. And the person who looks askance at these efforts is missing the boat on the recidivism solution. It is not just about recovery, unity, and service. It is about becoming whole—physically, mentally, and spiritually. About being honest, moral, unselfish children of the living Creator. These are what make the difference.

I have visited Dunklin Memorial Church in the swamps of Okeechobee, Florida, several times. People are taken there from prisons and jails and go there for religious, vocational, recovery, family, and accountability growth. They have been coached and loved by a "red neck" cowboy minister who founded the place in an alligator patch. The people work, attend religious training and services, and do some modified Twelve Step, Quiet Time, and recovery-type study. I have talked to several people who had been there for some months. I have heard their stories and then their testimonies. I have seen their eagerness for new lives. I have seen the members of their family who come to visit and support. And I have seen the love of God and of His children in action.

And there are many other efforts of this kind in Florida and elsewhere. Rev. Mickey Evans, the well-loved minister who set up Dunklin Memorial Church, was driving me around the Dunklin site. He spotted an aged man in the field and called out to him. Mickey was giving me a tour of his facility. He hollered to the oldster, "What do you know about A.A." The old guy said he had been in it for 50 years. Mickey asked him what he thought of it. The old man replied: "It's OK. But they do not know nothin' about God there. So we bring them here and teach them. Then everything goes just fine."

Help can be on the way in huge dimensions when people recognize *the Way*. And that Way is essential to the cure and the Godly life if it is to be experienced the way the founders experienced it in early A.A.

6
Facing "Reality" with "Divine Help"

Lots of us in A.A. talk about it as a "we" program. You cannot do it alone, we say. You do not need to do it alone, we say. Each group's primary purpose is to carry "the" message to someone who still suffers, we say. Alcoholics Anonymous is a fellowship of men and women who deal with their own problems and help others to stop drinking, we assert. But where's God in that message! What is the message if it is not about Almighty God, the Creator! What experience, strength, and hope do you have to share but the real and first A.A. message: "God has done for me what I could not do for myself." That one that caught Bill Wilson right between the eyes and launched his efforts to rely on the Creator and try to change his life. "Reality" is far too grim to face without the Creator at your side.

"Reality"

Twelve Step Fellowships today are loaded with self-made, compromise expressions. Some are faulty to the point of absurdity. Like, "Turn it over." Turn *what* over, and to *whom*! A light bulb or radiator? Another, "Just play with the cards that have been dealt you." In other words, abandon yourself to despair and make the best of a lousy hand. But what about Ephesians 3:20 as to God's ability to do exceeding abundantly beyond what you can ask or think? Then there is, "Welcome to reality." A "reality" that really means there is a big, bad world out there; and you just have to face it as it is. But what about 2 Corinthians 9:8 and God's ability to make all grace abound toward you that you, having all sufficiency in all things, may abound to every good work? Then you hear that, You just have to "accept"adversity. But what about Philippians 4:13 which states you can do all things through Christ which strengthens you? Also of some disaster, that "It was meant to be." Meant to be what! Meant by whom to be what. What about 1 Corinthians 10:13, which tells you that there is no temptation taken you but such as is common to man, but that God who is faithful will not suffer you to be tempted above that you are able, but will with the temptation also make a way to escape that ye may be able to bear it? "Acceptance is the answer," you hear. What about Romans 8:35-39 that tells you, as to tribulation, distress, nakedness, peril, or sword , that you are more than a conqueror through him that loved you.. "Acceptance" is only the answer if you believe that God cannot help you and ignore the fact that He expects you to use your mind, willpower, and best efforts—and to obey Him! Then, there is, "Willingness is the key." What does "willingness" mean? Does it mean "praying to be willing to become willing," as some confused people chant in meetings? Or does it mean to get off your hind end and move. There are a host of other self-defeating, dismal, vague, and compromising doormat ideas.

Just start with the Serenity Prayer. The first word is not "Serenity." It is not "acceptance." It is not "courage." It is not "change." It is God! Next look at the Lord's Prayer. The first words are not addressed to a "higher power." Nor a "light bulb." They are not about "acceptance." They are about "Our Father" with the kingdom and the power and the glory forever. Take a look at the Big Book's "turning point." It has to do with asking the Creator's protection and care with complete abandon. And what is the last of the three a,b,c's we hear read at so many meetings! The last one is: "God could and would if He were sought."

Dealing with "reality" means walking through life after establishing a relationship with Almighty God and then staying in fellowship with Him by seeing that the relationship is right and kept right. That is the substance of what the Big Book says to AAs if they read pages 29 and 164 with care.

Tossing out the "Nonsense gods" of Recovery

My latest title—published just before this one—is *God and Alcoholism: Our Growing Opportunity in the 21st Century*. It is about the original God-based program in the pioneer A.A. of the 1930's. It is about what God can do to heal us and cure us and deliver us and

Facing "Reality" with "Divine Help"   91

forgive us if we seek Him and ask Him according to His will. It is about receiving a cure instead of "recovering." It is about God instead of "not-god." It is about Divine Aid instead of treatment aid. And it is about rejecting the idolatry that permeates today's recovery thinking, speaking, and literature.

As Bill Wilson and Sam Shoemaker both put it: God either is, or He isn't. The Bible leaves no doubt that He is. It also leaves no doubt as to His will, His love, His healing power, and His forgiveness. The Good Book tells us His name—*Yahweh*. It tells us that His name is holy and not to be profaned. It tells us to have no other gods before Him. And it tells us there is one God—not an ever-multiplying group of chairs, tables, light bulbs, radiators, groups, and "Somethings."

If you want to help a newcomer—whether you are in or out of A.A.—just put the boot to the statement that the word "God" will drive a newcomer out of the rooms. It might if he is looking for an argument instead of help. It might if he is more concerned with what he *thinks* he believes than with what the Creator tells us to believe. It might if he hears one of today's many outspoken, irreligious members who have little to support their views other than a loud voice.

Show the newcomer the 400-plus times God is mentioned in the latest edition of A.A.'s Big Book. And in all the previous three editions. Show the newcomer the 12 times the Big Book refers to the Creator and the need for His presence. Show the newcomer my documented proof that A.A.'s basic ideas came from the Bible. Show the newcomer that Bill Wilson called the Creator "Almighty God." Show the newcomer that Dr. Bob Smith called the Creator "Your Heavenly Father." Show the newcomer that Jesus's sermon on the mount taught his listeners to pray to "Our Father." Show the newcomer that both Bill Wilson and Dr. Bob said that Jesus's "Sermon on the Mount" (Matthew chapters 5-7) contained the underlying A.A. philosophy. Learn the facts and use them. And then point out to the newcomer that there is not one word in the Big Book's basic text that suggests that the Creator Almighty God, Whose name is *Yahweh*, is, is called, or can possibly be called or described as a chair, a table, a self, a group, Ralph, Gertrude, Santa Claus, a radiator, or the Big Dipper. Not even an "it" or "nothing at all." Show the newcomer in A.A. literature exactly where and how Dr. Bob asked the important question, "Do you believe in God?" See *DR. BOB and the Good Oldtimers*. (NY: Alcoholics Anonymous World Services, Inc., 1980), p. 144. Show the newcomer the last page of Dr. Bob's story (Big Book, 4th ed., p. 181) where he says he felt sorry for the atheist, the agnostic, the skeptic, and the critic who did not want to accept the A.A. program as laid out in the Big Book.

If, as the Big Book states on page 43, the real alcoholic is 100% hopeless apart from Divine help, states elsewhere that he is *medically* incurable, and states further that it will therefore be talking about God, then who wants a radiator. Who wants to pray to a chair. Who thinks that removing "self" from the picture will pull in God without coming to Him through the Way..

The theme here is that the sooner the recovery community places itself in harmony with the medical community and the religious community—as A.A. was in the beginning—the sooner real healings and cures will be seen instead of disputed and denied.

Alcoholics May Be Sick, but They Are Not Stupid

Give the newcomer a break. He probably does not want to join A.A. He probably does not want to quit drinking. He probably does not want to go to meetings. And he probably thinks that AAs are religious squares. But he is not likely to walk through the doors believing that AAs think God is a chair. Give him a break.

Our U.S. coins and currency all say, "In God we trust." Our Pledge of Allegiance *still* contains the word "God." Our Armed Services administer oaths that end, "So help me God." Our Supreme Court opens with mention of God. Our Congress opens with prayers and displays the Ten Commandments. Our Declaration of Independence refers to the Creator. Our presidents take their oath of office with hand on the Bible. And we somehow think that newcomers are so stupid they will seek help from a radiator or Santa Claus instead of God. Most of them quit believing in Santa Claus long before they started drinking and using. Give them a break. You can decide never to propagandize an emerging newcomer with trash about higher powers and idolatrous door knobs and groups. Give them a break. Remind them where they came from. Ask them why we have Christmas. Ask them why we celebrate Easter. Ask them why our calendars say *A.D. (Anno Domini -the year of the Lord)* instead of B.C. (Before Christ). And do not doubt for a moment that even a sick, detoxing alkie can tell the difference between Gertrude and God. And will opt for God if he knows the founders of Alcoholics

Facing "Reality" with "Divine Help" 93

Anonymous insisted on His help and did not ask Gertrude for assistance—Gertrude being the "higher power" of one A.A. historian.

The Emphasis Needs to Be on Changing Their Lives

I like to say that God wouldn't have provided Ten Commandments if there hadn't been a problem about obedience. That He wouldn't have told us what *not* to do if we had not been doing it. That He wouldn't have told us we needed a new birth, to be born from above, to become new creatures, if the first, earthly birth, and the "old man nature" sufficed. Jesus flatly assured us of God's love in making everlasting life available (John 3:16). He wouldn't have made the point if we already had everlasting life. Jesus talked specifically about his coming to make an abundant life available (John 10:10). He wouldn't have done so if we already had it. Jesus spelled out the need for doing God's will (Matthew 7:20); and he wouldn't have done so if people were unerringly doing it.

If God and His Son told us we need to change, they wouldn't have done so if we did not need to change. They wouldn't have told us to stop sinning if we had stopped sinning. They wouldn't have told us to love God and love our brother if we were already doing so. And on, and on, and on, and on. There are commands in the Bible to love, not hate; to repent, not continue to sin; to become born again (of the spirit), not just be born of a woman; to believe, not just to fear. And on and on and on.

Pioneer A.A. called upon people to change. To change from evil to good, from lawlessness to lawfulness, from anger to love, from dishonesty to truthfulness, from greed to unselfishness, and from fear to belief in the power of God.

You can help. There is no excuse for having a fellowship of people who file no tax returns, drive without insurance or licenses, dodge arrest and court appearances, flee from creditors and courts, ignore child support, fail to forgive and amend, and on and on and on. That is not what either the Bible or the Oxford Group taught to early AAs. Yet many today do these things without criticism from the fellowship, despite the language of the Big Book; and they do it without being chastised within the fellowship. The Bible calls for truthfulness, honesty, justness, purity, love, and good conduct (Philippians 4:8). The Good Book rejects lies. It rejects hatred. Fornication and adultery are rejected. On the other hand, ministering to others is the standard. "Jesus Christ was a minister of the circumcision [the Jews] for the truth of God, to confirm the promises *made* unto the fathers" (Romans 15:8). Paul was "the minister of Jesus Christ to the Gentiles, ministering the gospel of God, that the offering up of the Gentiles might be acceptable, being sanctified by the Holy Ghost" (Romans 15:16; 3:28-30). So too the believers of the First Century Church (Acts 2:42-47; 4:32-37). All believers were called to become one body by accepting Christ (Ephesians 1:15; 2:16). To trust and serve the one, living, and true God (Ephesians 1:5-6; 1 Timothy 2:5; 1 Thessalonians 1:9; 1 Timothy 6:17). And by love to serve one another (Galatians 5:13; 1 Thessalonians 3:12; Romans 13:10; James 2:8).

Change from crime to lawfulness. Change from deception to truthfulness. Change from infidelity to faithfulness. Change from coveting to giving. All these were calls from God enjoining change by obeying His laws, and not just traveling the ways of men. And these were strongly espoused principles in early A.A. You can stress them today in your life and your witness to new people.

7
Talking Plainly about the Creator

The Bible is the best-selling book of all time. Religion has talked about the Creator and Christ for centuries. Churches of all denominations abound in our country. Kids are taught to "say their prayers." Yet the recovery fellowships of today are scared to death to mention *Yahweh* or His Son Jesus. There is no First Amendment in recovery, but there are First Amendment principles about free speech and no dictated church. Freedom to speak is as much a privilege in a recovery meeting as it is on a soap box in New York. Freedom to believe in God, to study the Bible, to accept Jesus as Lord, to seek a new birth, to talk about God's will, and to mention your faith and your church are as much a privilege in a recovery meeting as in the Army, in jail, in a court of law, and in a hospital. In fact, the Bible was the only book allowed AAs in the hospital in the pioneer days.

"Finding" God

God is not lost. Many AAs are. Reverend Sam Shoemaker was well known for his writings on "How to Find God" or "The Way to Find God." The way, of course, is to *seek Him.* The Big Book has that part right. But the way to seek Him is through His Son, Jesus Christ. And that way, according to Big Book teaching, requires you to eliminate self-centeredness. But that is *not* the way. The way is through being born again of God's spirit (John chapter 3). The way was made available through the crucifixion and death of Jesus Christ (John 3:16). The way was opened to all who want to believe that God raised Jesus from the dead. And to way to the new birth is through confession with your mouth that Jesus is Lord and belief in your heart that God did raise Jesus from the dead (Romans 10:9).

Talking about Almighty God

Sam Shoemaker wrote an apologia for his life. Many have titled it "I Stand by the Door." However, I discovered Sam's apologia pamphlet among his personal papers at the Episcopal Church Archives in Austin, Texas. And Sam actually titled his poem "I Stay Near the Door." Either way, Sam felt his life should be devoted to pointing the way through the door to God. And Sam never minced words about who God was, who Jesus Christ was, what the Bible had to say about each of them, and how to gain access to the Creator through believing on His Son Jesus Christ. That fact was so clear that Dr. Bob's wife, Anne Ripley Smith, wrote in her journal, and taught early AAs and their families, that replacing Christ with the "group" was one of the "funk holes." Anne wrote of such "funk holes":

> Unwillingness to use the word Christ. Talking about a house party without saying anything about your own personal defeats and how you faced up to Jesus Christ. Using the word "Group" instead of "Christ." [See Dick B., *Anne Smith's Journal, 1933-1939.* 3rd ed. (Kihei, HI: Paradise Research Publications, 1998), pp. 91-92.]

Whatever Anne's full implications in using the phrase "funk holes," I have no doubt that she meant that substituting "group" for "Christ" promulgated a false belief and false approach, in that it called a group "god." Nonetheless, see the following evidence that Bill W. introduced just such funk hole in his *Twelve Steps and Twelve Traditions* (NY: Alcoholics Anonymous World Services, 1952):

> You can, if you wish, make A.A. itself your "higher power" (p. 27).

> The more we become willing to depend upon a Higher Power, the more independent we actually are. Therefore dependence, as A.A. practices it, is really a means of gaining true independence of the spirit (p. 36).

> ... [D]ependence upon an A.A. group or upon a Higher Power hasn't produced any baleful results (p. 38).
>
> So how, exactly, can the willing person continue to turn his will and his life over to the Higher Power? . . . . His lone courage and unaided will cannot do it. Surely he must now depend upon Somebody or Something else (p. 39).

Wilson concludes this later-A.A. theological hodge podge by quoting the "Serenity Prayer"—which begins with "God"—and then paraphrasing the Bible's reference to God's will—"Thy will, not mine, be done."

Is it any wonder that Anne Smith called such Bible-dodging the path to "funk holes" and chose herself to write: "Of course, the Bible ought to be the main Source Book of all. No day ought to pass without reading it" (Dick B., *Anne Smith's Journal, supra*, p. 82). The A.A. pioneers studied the Word of God to learn about Almighty God—not to learn about an A.A. group, a higher power, a Somebody, or a Something else. And it is important to pass that information along when you are talking about God. Cures, in Pioneer A.A., were sought from *Yahweh. Not from a group, a Somebody, a Something, or a chair that had been dubbed by some Buddhist as a "higher power."*

The Basic Text Is the Bible.
"Back to Basics" Means Back to the Bible

You can invent or reconstruct or report on any supposed program of A.A. that you want. And for any period after 1938 that you wish to select. You can call it the "basics." But Dr. Bob said that A.A.'s *basic ideas* came from study of the Bible. And if you want the straight scoop on the Creator, here are some pointers about Him from the Good Book:

- God created the heavens and the earth (Genesis 1:1). He is the Creator.

- God has a proper, personal name [Exodus 3:15; 6:2,3; Isa. 42:8; Jer. 16:21; Ps. 83:18 (*Jerusalem Bible*; *Rotherham's Emphasized Bible*)]. His name is *Yahweh.*

- There is but one God (Ephesians 4:6; 1 Timothy 2:5).

- We are to have no other gods before Yahweh our God (Exodus 10:3); and we are to turn to God from idols to serve the living and true God (1 Thessalonians 1:9).

- To come to God, we must believe that He is, and that He is a rewarder of them that diligently seek Him (Hebrews 11:6).

- God said: I am the Lord that healeth thee (Exodus 15:26).

- God is love (1 John 4:8, 16).

- Yahweh our God forgives all our iniquities, heals all our diseases, and redeems our lives from destruction (Psalm 103:3-4).

- The Bible states: "Herein is love, not that we loved God, but that he loved us, and sent his Son to be the propitiation for our sins" (1 John 4:10). It also states: "[T]he Father sent the Son to be the Saviour of the world" (1 John 4:14).

- The Lord our God's first and great commandment is to love Him with all our heart and with all our soul and with all our mind; and the second is to love thy neighbor as thyself. On these two commandments hang all the law and the prophets (Cf. Matthew 22:36-40).

- "For this is the love of God, that we keep His commandments" (1 John 5:3a).

- Love is defined, in part, in 1 Corinthians 13:4-7.

- God's will is for all men to be saved and to come unto the knowledge of the truth (1 Timothy 2:3-4).

- God's only begotten Son is the way, the truth, and the life; and no man comes unto the Father but by God's Son, Jesus Christ (John 14:6).

Talking Plainly about the Creator 99

- In simple words, God assures you that you shall be saved if you confess with your mouth that Jesus is Lord and believe in your heart that God raised Jesus from the dead (Romans 10:9).

- The Apostle Peter stated by revelation that there is no name under heaven given among men than the name of Jesus Christ of Nazareth by which we must be saved (Acts 4:10-12).

- The record is: that God hath given to us eternal life, and this life is in his Son. He that hath the Son hath life; and he that hath not the Son of God hath not life (1 John 5:11-12).

- Jesus Christ declared that God's word "is truth" (John 17:17).

- The Bible states: "And whatsoever we ask, we receive of him, because we keep his commandments, and do those things that are pleasing in his sight. And this is his commandment, That we should believe on the name of his Son Jesus Christ, and love one another, as he gave us commandment" (1 John 3:22-23).

- The Bible also states: "And this is the confidence that we have in him, that, if we ask any thing according to His will, he heareth us: And if we know that he hear us, whatsoever we ask, we know that we have the petitions that we desired of him" (1 John 5:14-15).

- The Apostle Paul by revelation stated: Study to shew thyself approved unto God, a workman that needeth not to be ashamed, rightly dividing the word of truth (2 Timothy 2:15).

God heals and cures all diseases. He says so, and that should settle it for the believer. Alcoholics need the simple truths in the Bible about what God has done, can do, promises to do, and will do if we obey His will and believe. And my book *God and Alcoholism* cites verse after verse stating those truths from the Bible. My book *God and Alcoholism* also specifically points to all those who have believed and testify to these facts—including the founders of Alcoholics Anonymous!

Alcoholics should not be told they cannot be cured. They should be told they can be cured. They should be told their founders were cured. Those founders were cured by the Creator! Bill Wilson, Dr. Bob, and Bill Dotson all said so—explicitly, many times (See Big Book, 4th ed., pp. 181, 191). And we will deal with that cure in a moment. But cured they were, for sure!

You can be cured if you are an alcoholic. You can help someone to a cure if he is an alcoholic. I have been cured; and I believed the Bible accounts that confirmed the availability of a cure. For example, consider these points: (1) If alcoholism is a sin, then that is a sin I no longer commit or want to commit or have to commit—ever again. (2) If alcoholism is a disease, then I have been healed. God heals all diseases (Psalm 103:1, 3; 2 Kings 20:5; Jeremiah 30:17). (3) If alcoholism is an infirmity or illness or the result of evil spirits, then I have been cured. God cures all infirmities and diseases (Jeremiah 33:6; Luke 7:21; Luke 9:1; Luke 13:22; John 5:8-10). Whatever science, medicine, or religion may choose to call the result, I submitted myself to God, resisted the devil, and he took a hike. God lifted me! (James 4:7, 10).

That is what alcoholics should be told, and that is what I tell them if I am working with them. That is what Jerry Dunn told over 500,000 readers of his book *God Is for the Alcoholic;* and I have met Jerry Dunn at a conference where I shared the platform with him. I heard his story. I later read his book. He had been healed and lifted out of his alcoholism and all the misery that had gone with it. That is what alcoholics should be told, and that is what he tells them. We can all tell them that.

8
There Is More to Cure Than Abstinence

God save us from the alcoholic who is merely hanging on to an A.A. seat, lying to himself and others, and refraining from a drink—one day at a time. An alcoholic can be miserable without a drink when he is stone, cold, sober. If he has not been cured, that is. And there is more—far more—to the cure than being "recovered" with only a daily reprieve. Lots more. But let's talk first about the misery.

Casting out the Misery

There are physical remnants of his drinking days that can leave the "recovered" alcoholic quite miserable—liver ailments, shakes, insomnia, pain, incontinence, and so on. There are mental remnants too—brain damage, confusion, guilt, fear, anger, depression, shame, low self-esteem, suicidal thoughts, hopelessness. Then there are all the other elements of the wreckage—criminal, civil, marital, family, debt, divorce, abuse, injuries, homelessness, joblessness, rejection, retaliation. And many more as well.

The end of drinking often spells the beginning of misery. It did for me. I wasn't happy in those last nine months of drinking. But I believe I was far less agitated, fearful, angry, depressed, sleepless, forgetful, confused, bewildered, lonely, and anxious than when I first quit drinking. Then came A.A. Detoxing came first. Depression came next. Then fear became the worst adversary. Insomnia lasted for a very long time; so did the shaking; so did the forgetfulness and confusion. And that was not living! Furthermore, if that was recovery, it did not cut it for me. I was still defeated, licked, and hopeless—or so I thought.

The more the troubles lasted, the more I realized how badly I needed God's help and forgiveness and healing. Education was not a problem. Physical ill health was not really a problem. Finances were not a real problem. Alienation was! Where were my family members. Where were my colleagues. Where were my friends. Where were the AAs and my sponsor. I was alone and frightened and intimidated. I felt the game was over and that I needed the Veterans Home at Yountville, California. I secured an application. It asked if I had an alcohol problem or had been treated for one. I did and I had. It asked if I had mental problems or had been treated for them. I did and was in the VA psych ward at that very moment. It asked if I had a criminal record. I did not have one yet; but I was scheduled to plead guilty to a felony. Hence I could not even get in the Veterans Home!

There may be many like me. Like I felt myself to be, they may feel defeated by fear and despair. They may be defeated by recidivism. They may be defeated by unemployment. They may be defeated by the law or by family problems. They may be defeated by debt. They may be defeated by loneliness and feelings of worthlessness and failure. They may see no light at the end of the tunnel. For these and for many others who have gone the alcoholic and addict route, the road back can and should start with reliance on God and learning the *basics and the advanced* ideas from the Bible.

The Freedom, Provided by God

What God has done is, of course, miraculous. What God can do may seem unbelievable. What God promises to do for those who believe Him, love Him, and obey Him is boundless. The angel told Mary as to Jesus's birth: "For with God nothing shall be impossible" (Luke 1:37). Countless Bible accounts back that up. Blind healed. Deaf and dumb given back their hearing and speech. Leprosy healed. Mental illness eradicated. Lame people cured. Dead people raised. Evil spirits cast out. Signs, miracles, and wonders at every turn (See Mark 16:10-20). The Old Testament hall of fame as recounted in Hebrews is enough to keep anyone amazed. Can God do these things for the alcoholic, for you, for your family or friends?

I believe each of my many titles has a special message of its own. [See particularly, Dick B. *Why Early A.A. Succeeded: The Good Book in Alcoholics Anonymous Yesterday and Today (A Bible Study Primer for AAs and other 12-Steppers)*. (Kihei, HI: Paradise Research

There Is More to Cure Than Abstinence

Publications, 2001).] In that title is an example of a particular, special message. I very much wanted to show there what the Bible said about the releases available to one who seeks God's help. And I remind you that there was a good deal of talk about *release* in the early A.A. days:

The Freedom Claimed by Pioneers

Of the cure of Rowland Hazard, the Oxford Group activist who really started the whole ball rolling, Bill Wilson wrote:

> But this man still lives, and is a free man. He does not need a bodyguard nor is he confined. He can go anywhere on this earth where other free men may go without disaster. . . he had the extraordinary experience, which, as we have already told you, made him a free man [*Alcoholics Anonymous*, 4th ed., pp. 28-29].

Of the freedom received by Ebby Thacher, Bill's former drinking friend and "sponsor," A.A. Number One Bill Wilson. wrote:

> The door opened and he stood there, fresh-skinned and glowing. There was something about his eyes. He was inexplicably different. What had happened? . . . He looked straight at me. Simply, but smilingly, he said, "I've got religion" . . . and he made the point-blank declaration that God had done for him what he could not do for himself. His human will had failed. Doctors had pronounced him incurable. Society was about to lock him up. Like myself, he had admitted complete defeat. Then he had, in effect, been raised from the dead, suddenly taken from the scrap heap to a level of life better than the best he had ever known! [*Alcoholics Anonymous*, 4th ed, pp. 9-11].

Of his own cure, A.A. Number One, Bill Wilson, wrote:

> There was a sense of victory, followed by such a peace and serenity as I had ever known. There was utter confidence. I felt lifted up, as though the great clean wind of a mountain top blew through and through. God comes to most men gradually, but His impact on me was sudden and profound [*Alcoholics Anonymous*, 4th ed., p. 14].

Later, after Bill Dotson had been cured, Bill Wilson said:

> Henrietta, the Lord has been so wonderful to me, curing me of this terrible disease, that I just wanted to keep talking about it and telling people [*Alcoholics Anonymous*, 4th ed., p. 191].

A.A. Number Two, Dr. Bob Smith, wrote this of his cure:

> It is a most wonderful blessing to be relieved of the terrible curse with which I was afflicted. My health is good and I have regained my self-respect and the respect of my colleagues. My home life is ideal and my business is as good as can be expected in these uncertain times. I spend a great deal of time passing on what I learned to others who want and need it badly [*Alcoholics Anonymous*, 4th ed., p. 180].

Speaking of A.A. Number Three's *immediate* recovery and cure, Bill Wilson said:

> Bill D. walked out of that hospital a free man, never to drink again" [*Alcoholics Anonymous*, 4th ed., p. 189].

Saying that Bill Wilson's expression about the Lord's curing him had actually become a golden text for him (Bill Dotson) and for A.A., Dotson said:

> . . . I did come to the conclusion that I was willing to put everything I had into it, with God's power, and that I wanted to do just that. As soon as I had done that, I did feel great release" [*Alcoholics Anonymous*, 4th ed., p. 189].

"Fitz"—John Henry Fitzhugh Mayo—an Episcopalian, and the son of an Episcopalian minister, was one of the few in earliest New York days, to get sober and stay sober; and he wrote of his experience as follows:

> *Who are you to say there is no God?* . . . I tumble out of bed onto my knees. I know not what I say. But slowly a great peace comes to me. I feel lifted up. I believe in God. I crawl back into bed and sleep like a child [*Alcoholics Anonymous*, 4th ed., pp. 55-57, 215-18].

God Lifts You

Most assuredly, there is more, far more involved than just "release" and "freedom," where there has been cure, an abundant life, and everlasting life. But my own experience, and that of so many of the early AAs who really turned to, and relied on the Creator, was that of being lifted out of the mire. It was and is the freedom that comes from learning and knowing the truth about God from the Good Book. That truth shall make you free. There are countless releases immediately available to the born again believer. Those releases you can receive are also covered in my title *Why Early A.A. Succeeded*, pp. 153-70, and in the Bible. I call them, as a group, "release from your prisons;" and here are some:

Release from *Your* Prisons

A Release through the Promises, Works, and Accomplishments of Jesus Christ

> Verily, verily, I say unto you, He that believeth on me, the works that I do shall he do also; and greater works than these shall he do; because I go unto my Father. And whatsoever ye shall ask in my name, that will I do, that the Father may be glorified in the Son (John 14:12-13).

> Then Jesus said to those Jews which believed on him, If ye continue in my word, *then* are ye my disciples indeed; and ye shall know the truth, and the truth shall make you free. If the Son therefore shall make you free, ye shall be free indeed (John 8:31-32, 36).

> Giving thanks unto the Father, which hath made us meet to be partakers of the inheritance of the saints in light: Who hath delivered us from the power of darkness, and hath translated us into the kingdom of his dear Son (Colossians 1:12-13).

Power

> And, behold, I send the promise of my Father upon you: but tarry ye in the city of Jerusalem, until ye be endued with power from on high (Luke 24:49).

Above All That We Ask or Think

> Now unto him that is able to do exceeding abundantly above all that we ask or think, according to the power that worketh in us (Ephesians 3:20).

Believing in Order to Receive

> For this cause also thank we God without ceasing, because, when ye received the word of God, which ye heard of us, ye received it not *as* the word of men, but as it is in truth, the word of God, which effectually worketh also in you that believe (1 Thessalonians 2:13).

Forgiveness, Healing, Deliverance, Kindness, and Mercy Are Some of God's Promises

> Bless the LORD [Yahweh], O my soul, and forget not all his benefits: Who forgiveth all thine iniquities; who healeth all thy diseases; Who redeemeth thy life from destruction: who crowneth thee with loving kindness and tender mercies (Psalm 103:2-4).

Release from Fear

> The fear of man bringeth a snare: but whoso putteth his trust in the LORD [*Yahweh*] shall be safe (Proverbs 29:25).

Release from Guilt

> There is therefore no condemnation to them which are in Christ Jesus.... (Romans 8:1).

Release from Anxiety.

> Be careful for [or "anxious about"] nothing; but in every thing by prayer and supplication with thanksgiving let your requests be made known unto God. And the peace of God, which passeth all understanding, shall keep your hearts and minds through Christ Jesus (Philippians 4:6-7).

Release from Shame

> According as he hath chosen us in him before the foundation of the world, that we should be holy and without blame before him in love (Ephesians 1:4).

Release from Insecurity

> But seek ye first the kingdom of God, and his righteousness; and all these things [food, clothing, shelter] shall be added unto you (Matthew 6:33).

Release from Poverty

> The blessing of the LORD [*Yahweh*], it maketh rich, and he addeth no sorrow with it (Proverbs 10:22).

Release from Cares

> Casting all your care upon him; for he careth for you (1 Peter 5:7).

Release from Confusion

> Thou wilt keep *him* in perfect peace, *whose* mind is stayed on *thee*: because he trusteth in thee (Isaiah 26:3)

Release from Weakness

> I can do all things through Christ which strengtheneth me (Philippians 4:13).

Release from Doubt

> If any of you lack wisdom, let him ask of God, that giveth to all men liberally, and upbraideth not; and it shall be given him. But let him ask in faith, nothing wavering. For he that wavereth is like a wave of the sea driven with the wind and tossed. For let not that man think that he shall receive anything of the Lord. A double minded man is unstable in all his ways (James 1:5-8).

Release from Temptation

> There hath no temptation taken you but such as is common to man: but God is faithful, who will not suffer you to be tempted above that ye are able; but will with the temptation also make a way to escape, that ye may be able to bear it (1 Corinthians 10:13).

Release from Disease

> How God anointed Jesus of Nazareth with the Holy Ghost and with power: who went about doing good, and healing all that were oppressed of the devil; for God was with him (Acts 10:38).

Everlasting Release

> For God so loved the world, that he gave his only begotten Son, that whosoever believeth in him should not perish, but have everlasting life (John 3:16).

And Much, Much More in the Good Book

The foregoing are certainly not, nor are they intended to be, a complete list of what God promises and what His Son accomplished for those who want to believe. You can find some of them, and more, in the Gideon Bible that sits in the drawer of your hotel room. You can find some of them, and more, in *The Runner's Bible*—in topical form—as subjects and verses about those subjects that Dr. Bob studied and recommended to so many. You certainly can find them in church and religious tracts, in Bible study guides, and in daily devotionals. In fact, there is probably not a single one that cannot be found in the four years of quarterly *The Upper Room* pamphlets that AAs regularly read from 1935 to 1939.

I listed above the ones that were so very useful to me in getting well in Alcoholics Anonymous. They cover many of the fears, guilts, shames, and sicknesses you find discussed in treatment materials. Yet they offer a guaranteed solution, instead of a life full of self-rejection and loathing. I needed to know that Jesus Christ had paid the price for me. I needed to believe that. And I stress it to those I try to help to enable them to get out of the ditch a lot faster than I did. And here is the simple payoff:

There Is More to Cure Than Abstinence   109

> What shall we then say to these things? If God *be* for us, who *can be* against us? He that spared not his own Son, but delivered him up for us all, how shall he not with him also freely give us all things? Who shall lay any thing to the charge of God's elect? *It is* God that justifieth. Who *is* he that condemneth. *It is* Christ that died, ye rather, that is risen again, who is even at the right hand of God, who also maketh intercession for us. Who shall separate us from the love of Christ? *shall* tribulation, or distress, or persecution, or famine, or nakedness, or peril, or sword?
> Nay, in all these things we are more than conquerors through him that loved us (Romans 8:31-35, 37).

> The Lord knoweth how to deliver the godly out of temptations, and to reserve the unjust unto the day of judgment to be punished (2 Peter 2:9).

> For the eyes of the Lord *are* over the righteous, and his ears *are open* unto their prayers: but the face of the Lord *is* against them that do evil. And who *is* he that will harm you, if ye be followers of that which is good? (1 Peter 3:12).

> Submit yourselves therefore to God. Resist the devil, and he will flee from you. Draw nigh to God, and he will draw nigh to you. Cleanse your hands, ye sinners; and purify your hearts, ye double minded. . . . Humble yourselves in the sight of the Lord, and he shall lift you up (James 4:7-8, 10).

As Reverend Sam Shoemaker wrote, particularly with reference to the Seventh Step, many of us need a kind of "Divine Derrick" to lift us up and out. And it is God who does the lifting as and when we obey Him.

Toss out the Blame; Change Yourself; and Walk in God's Ways

Free from Condemnation

You can be sober as a judge and be miserable—all at the same time. If you, or someone you are trying to help, is constantly blaming himself, loathing himself, fearing disclosure, and covering up, you can point to the fact that Jesus Christ came to eliminate that kind of fault-finding. He paid the price. You are washed free when you accept him and believe what he accomplished for you. From that point on, it is what you put in your mind, your mouth, and your actions. Are you a son of God, or are you the skunk you feel like? God's kids are washed and clean. Believe it.

It is one thing to adopt the Oxford Group and A.A. philosophy of self-examination and looking for your part in wrongdoing. It is quite another to claim ownership of a guilt complex. We are *justified (acquitted) by God*, not by what we think or do. We were redeemed by what Jesus *did* for us, not by our *works*. Some have phrased it this way: Religion is about "do." Christianity is about "done." We are righteous because God makes us righteous, not because of our good deeds.

Blame goes out the window with the new birth. Bad conduct does not. So what about the bad conduct?

The Duty to Change and Obey

God tells us to change and do His will. Not just to be sorry and blame ourselves or others.

> For godly sorrow worketh repentance to salvation not to be repented of; but the sorrow of the world worketh death (2 Corinthians 7:10).

> Knowing that a man is not justified by the works of the law, but by the faith of Jesus Christ, even we have believed in Jesus Christ, that we might be justified by the faith of Christ, and not by the works of the law: for by the works of the law shall no flesh be justified (Galatians 2:16)

> Casting down imaginations, and every high thing that exalteth itself against the knowledge of God, and bringing into captivity every thought to the obedience of Christ (2 Corinthians 10:5)

> That we should be to the praise of his glory, who first trusted in Christ. In whom ye also *trusted*, after that ye heard the word of truth, the gospel of your salvation: in whom also after that ye believed, ye were sealed with that holy Spirit of promise (Ephesians 1:12-13).

> If so be that ye have heard him, and have been taught by him, as the truth is in Jesus: That ye put off concerning the former

conversation the old man, which is corrupt according to the deceitful lusts; And be renewed in the spirit of your mind. And that ye put on the new man, which after God is created in righteousness and true holiness (Ephesians 4:21-25).

Page after page of the Gospels, the Book of Acts, and the Church Epistles tell us just what we are to put in our minds from the word of God—and do! That is the message that will change the life and lift the man. Learn what God wants. Put that in your mind. Believe what He commands. Confess that in your own words. And be "doers of the word and not hearers only" (James 1:22).

Practical Means of Avoiding Self-destruction

Much of what the cured person does with his every-day life and with his "spare" time makes a difference in whether or not his interests are turned away from self-destructive behavior. And there are Godly objectives which can help him avoid the detours.

Focus on Family

Healthy family, spousal, and child interrelationships are a vital part of a new life. The Bible lays down plenty of material on the subject; and so do clergy, churches, family organizations, youth activities, counselors, and non-profit agencies.

Avoidance of "Hostage-Taking"

The old alcoholic technique of "buying" friends, sequestering partners, and seeking meaningless "relationships" holds little promise for marriage, family, children, and friends. The idea that we should "love" people, not simply "use" them, is a good place to start.

Adequate Education

Those of us who try to help people "in recovery" soon become painfully aware of educational shortcomings: people who cannot read effectively, write effectively, spell properly, or speak articulately are common fare. So are those who dropped out of school, failed to get their diplomas, dumped their dreams of college, and failed to be challenged by prospects of professional careers in business, accounting, engineering, science, law, nursing, medicine, dentistry, architecture, and so on. The concept that homelessness, joblessness, uselessness, and hopelessness are acceptable goals just needs to be replaced with the promise and skills offered by education.

Meaningful Employment

Rare is the newly recovered alcoholic or addict who really has a stable job situation or employment record. Job training, job seeking, job changing, vocational rehabilitation, and restoration of self-esteem are usually areas where help is required.

Appropriate Housing

Finding a wholesome living place is an acute problem at the beginning. The alcoholic may have amassed a bad credit record, a bad tenancy record, a bad employment record, a bad attitude, and so on. His solution does not lie in treatment programs, rehabs, or half-way houses. All these end, and few of them equip him for the right kind of living atmosphere. He needs help, and you can supply it from time to time.

Proper Stewardship of Finances

The most difficult hurdle for those who help the alcoholic is learning how to say, "no." No to lending money. No to letting them near your telephone. No to leaving them alone in your house. No to letting them use your car. And so on. Typically, the new person, and many older members of the society, are always on the make for money. The problem in that quest is not so much a problem of finances as of honesty, integrity, accountability, and responsibility. It seems harsh to "just say no" to requests like the foregoing. But, unless you want to become a source for personal philanthropy, you will be disappointed over and over and over again if you do not require the alcoholic to go to God first, then to help himself, and only then to ask for your help.

Acquiring and Using Proper Social Skills

Courtesy, consideration, and kindness are not the long-suit of someone who has emerged from the depth. Nor is etiquette. Yet good behavior, good speech, and good will are part of a biblical success requirement and quality life. Bad behavior, if ignored, will continue. Reproof and correction, if presented in love, can do much to help the "bad" person become "good."

Cultivating Wholesome Fellowship and Companionship

Fellowship with like-minded believers is part and parcel of Christian teaching and practices found in the Gospels, the Book of Acts, and the "churches" held in houses and to which Paul often refers. Keeping company with those who believe in God, Jesus Christ, and the Bible is a commandment of God; and it keeps the believer focused—in thought, word, and deed—on the true will of God, as spelled out in the Bible and by revelation.

Some Real Basics

He is not a true well-wisher who tries to fluff off someone by sending him to meetings, telling him to go off and read the Big Book, telling him to put the Bible and all other reading on the shelf for a year, and advising him to "keep it simple" by just going to meetings and not drinking in between. Yet this is commonplace. It happened to me. The basics involve, for me, all the suggestions I have made above, coupled with the following additional basic guides.

"First Things First" Means God Comes First!

The first basic is reliance on Almighty God and doing His will. Genesis 1 commences with God. So should anyone who wants God's help and knows it comes through obedience to His will.

Then, "Three D's"—Decision, Determination, Discipline

The person seeking a cure has to make a decision. The decision is to quit drinking and drugging—once and for all. Then he must be determined to do whatever it takes to implement the decision. And he himself must establish, with God's help, the discipline of actually doing what he has decided to do and remain determined to succeed at it.

Receiving Accurate Bible and Big Book Training

Success does not come without learning. There is little to be expected from ignoring the Bible, ignoring the Big Book, ignoring the Steps, making up your own god, making up some absurd name for God, fashioning some half-baked prayers, and standing on some self-made religion. There is nothing in A.A. to suggest that this helter-skelter approach produces much besides disquiet, disaster, and drinking. In fact, when Reverend Sam Shoemaker addressed A.A.'s Convention, he decried "half-baked prayers" and "absurd names for God." And Shoemaker rejected "self-help" movements and "self-made religion" in a number of his writings.

The Bible needs to be taught, and it was taught in the Oxford Group, in Shoemaker's church and meetings, and in Akron A.A. In each case, it was taught by competent teachers. I personally believe strongly that the Big Book needs to be taught. I wandered aimlessly through meeting after meeting where I got sober and could not seem to get correct information on the Big Book or how to "take" the Steps according to its directions. Then I was steered to a "Joe and Charlie Big Book Seminar," where I finally got excellent direction on the Big Book and the Steps. The A.A. program, as such, finally came alive for me. And I know that I was enabled to teach the Big Book properly to many many men and to take them through the Twelve Steps in accordance with instructions in the Big Book.

Learning Responsibility

You cannot "fix" the alcoholic. Long hard experience and failure have proved that point in A.A., in treatment, in therapy, in jails, and in bookstores. The key is not forcing recovery on someone. It is expecting and receiving an assumption of responsibility on the part of the one who wants to be cured. The alcoholic has to want to be cured. He has to decide to be cured. He must be determined to be cured. And he must discipline himself to the cure and to a successful life after cure. In one word, he must be *responsible for his own cure.* You are not. God can help, but the alcoholic must act! If the Bible

There Is More to Cure Than Abstinence 115

commands one not to drink excessively, that is God's command; but it is the alcoholic who must, with God's help, stop his excessive drinking.

Drunk driving classes, alcohol information classes, treatment classes, therapy groups, "basics" classes, and meetings will not stop an alcoholic from drinking or cure him. As a matter of fact, these often furnish the alcoholic with an "excuse" to justify continued drinking. "It just won't work for me," he often says. Yet he is the one responsible for seeking God, for praying, and for taking the action to quit for good.

Real Survival, Purpose, Growth, Accomplishment

It is hard to convince the alcoholic or addict that he is in a battle for survival. We all hear it. The Big Book talks about it. There are dire threats that if the self-destructive behavior continues, it leads to death, insanity, or prison. But risk-taking seems to be part of the game. You cannot tell a big game hunter, he might get eaten. You cannot tell a racing car driver that he might be killed in a crash. You cannot tell a smoker he is sure to die of cancer or heart disease. Nor can you tell an alcoholic he may die, go insane, or go to jail. Chances are, he has been very close to all three, many times. But survival versus assured failure is one element of the decision process.

There has to be a purpose to it all. The despondent, homeless, sick person does not exert the self-will it takes to get well if he thinks he never will get well, never will get over his troubles, and never will attain a normal life. It is the stories of "experience, strength, *and hope*" that supposedly motivate recovery. I am not sure this is true because such stories may and do often cause the suffering person to conclude that he is "not that bad" or somehow beyond help. But adding a solid purpose to the required effort is one element of the "Three D" process.

In the Big Book Seminars, Joe and Charlie often say that you are either growing or dying. True or false, one of the spurs to determined effort is the belief that you are making *progress*. The swimmer that makes it through the first competition, the golfer who survives the cut, the racer who's running a faster mile often find the determination and discipline to go on from the progress already made. They are encouraged. They need to be encouraged. And they welcome evidence of growth and progress.

Receiving "chips" or medallions is one real token of accomplishment for the person on the way up and out. Not if he fails a dozen times, but when he gets his first "30 day chip," his "ninety day chip," his "sixth month chip," and the big "ONE"—sober for a year chip. Knowing that you decided to arrive, put out the effort to arrive, and finally made it is one of the basics of great importance.

Spiritual Relationship and Fellowship with the Father and His Son

All the training, motivation, encouragement, and reward techniques in the world do not hold a candle to what you receive when you are born again, become one of God's kids, and manifest the power of God the Father gives you. These all involve God's will and rest on obedience to His will. But healing, forgiveness, and deliverance are something God not only gives, but something you can take to the bank. God lifts you. And you know it. The following are assurances from God:

> Be careful [anxious] for nothing; but in everything by prayer and supplication with thanksgiving let your requests be known unto God. And the peace of God, which passeth all understanding, shall keep your hearts and minds through Christ Jesus (Philippians 4:6-8).
>
> Humble yourselves in the sight of the Lord, and he shall lift you up (James 4:10).
>
> And the prayer of faith shall save the sick, and the Lord shall raise him up; and if he have committed sins, they shall be forgiven him. Confess *your* faults one to another, and pray for one another, that ye may be healed. The effectual fervent prayer of a righteous man availeth much (James 5:15-16).
>
> But the God of all grace, who hath called us unto his eternal glory by Christ Jesus, after that ye have suffered a while, make you perfect, stablish, strengthen, settle *you* (1 Peter 5:10).
>
> That which was from the beginning, which we have heard, which we have seen with our eyes, which we have looked upon, and our hands have handled, of the Word of life; (For the life was manifested, and we have seen *it*, and bear witness, and shew unto

you that eternal life, which was with the Father, and was manifested unto us;) That which we have seen and heard declare we unto you, that ye also may have fellowship with us: and truly our fellowship *is* with the Father, and with his Son Jesus Christ. And these things write we unto you, that your joy may be full (1 John 1:1-4).

... God is love; and he that dwelleth in love dwelleth in God, and God in him.... There is no fear in love; but perfect love casteth out fear: because fear hath torment. He that feareth is not made perfect in love (1 John 4:16, 18).

Beloved, I wish above all things that thou mayest prosper and be in health, even as thy soul prospereth (3 John 2).

9
My Own Table of Tips

I sure do not have all the answers; not by a long shot. There are old-timers still around who have dealt with wet drunks, disasters, disease, despair, depression, and "relapses." They have many practical ideas about how to work with a newcomer. But this book is about being cured by the power of God. And it is about how you, as one who wants to be cured or as one who wants to help someone to cure, can meet and face the problems the way that I did.

What Has Worked Best

Seeking out the Newcomer

The new man does not come to you. He just does not bounce in the door and select the person who is going to help him. If you *are* the new man, you *seek out* your helper if he does not come to you. But if you are in the fellowship, it is your job to go newcomer netting. At every function. At every meeting. And at every opportunity. I have already discussed the approaches at a meeting. But there is so much more. If you are going to a movie, a dance, a retreat, a birthday party, a convention, a camp out, a sports event, a coffee store, or whatever, bring along a newcomer. It is a must. The essence of selfishness in A.A. is to go to an event with a girl or a friend or another AA and never reach out to a newcomer. That is not the way it is done.

Establishing Confidence

There will be no success if you do not personalize your interest in the new person. I have already discussed some techniques. But the drunk will never dive in and go for recovery if the water is icy. Everyone has his own way of showing he cares. But I like the phrase one of my sponsees gave me (and he is a gem at working with new people): "No one cares how much you know until they know how much you care." I remember that, right after I entered A.A. and had seizures, my new sponsor visited my hospital room at ICU without my knowing it. But when I came to, there was a small vase of flowers next to my bed with a note of support. It tied me to him even during the subsequent period in a treatment program!

Qualifying the Newcomer As One Who Wants *Your* Help

Alkies are pros at borrowing, stealing, cheating, lying, rationalizing, boasting, covering, procrastinating, making lame excuses, isolating, and using a hundred other techniques to obscure uncertainty or unwillingness or fear. It is not a part of their genes, but it has often been a part of unsuccessful survival behavior. And there will be little progress, and almost certain failure, if you cannot persuade them of the seriousness of the problem, the program, and the potential. You cannot be sure from their answers, but you have to try for their *commitment:* (1) Do they know they have a drinking or drug problem. (2) Do they want to do something about it. (3) Do they understand that most, if not all, of their difficulties have arisen out of alcoholism and addiction. (4) Do they know just how certain are the adverse consequences of continuing—incarceration, insanity, and death (we often are told). (5) Do they know what an "alcoholic" is and how to find out if they are an alcoholic. (6) Have they tried other ways unsuccessfully. (7) Do they see some light at the end of the tunnel if they successfully quit. (8) Are they willing to go to any lengths, to do what it takes, to put everything into the effort to quit. (9) Do they accept the fact that they are quitting *forever*; that the A.A. way means total abstinence—for good; and that life can be lived without drinking or drugging. (10) Will they follow directions completely—come with the winners, go where they go, do what they do, and try to "get" what they have got. (11) Will they give the program everything they have got.

My Own Table of Tips

Now, there is no one alive who will truthfully say "yes" to all the foregoing points. And there are many lazy ways to put them across. Also some good ones. You can tell them: "Don't drink, and go to meetings." That is not a formula for success. You can tell them to "Read the Doctor's Opinion and the first 164 pages of the Big Book." Yet most of them will not understand or remember what they are reading. You can tell them to come see you once a week in order to study the Big Book and take the Steps. But they are lonely, fearful, confused, and hesitant.

I believe there are some important keys: (1) You can obtain good responses from the new person if you share from your own experiences. This builds confidence and truthfulness and gains acquiescence. (2) You can inject humor into their stories and yours. (3) You can let them know you are with them all the way if they will follow. (4) You can give them some rules of the road and tell them they must follow them if they want to work with you. (5) You can administer a test like the "Twenty Questions" and compare their answers with yours. (6) As stated, the most important starting place, is to get them to tell you their story and share yours with them when appropriate. (7) You can tell them exactly what is expected of them and what you did—good or bad. (8) You can be their companion and not just their teacher.

There are some important survival rules for early sobriety, I have found most helpful: (1) You ask them to phone you whenever they need to—day or night—and at least once a day. (2) You tell them to get other phone numbers and call people just to say hello and keep in touch. (3) You tell them to go to meetings frequently—good ones; and you go with them. (4) You let them know they are part of a team—others you are working with. (5) You give them encouragement wherever appropriate and possible. (6) You introduce them to successful people in the fellowship. (7) You do what you can to help them with their problems or put them in touch with someone who can help—whether the problems are medical, mental, financial, necessities, legal, criminal, or religious. (8) You tell them to participate in the fellowship in whatever way they can—whether it is greeting, making coffee, setting up chairs, and the like and that they need to make as many friends as they can among the people who are active and serious. (9) You tell them to fill their hours with sober and drug-free activities—things that successful members are either doing, or have told them about.

My view is that if you do not want to be bothered with a new person, or be bothered by a new person, or bother to give him full instruction and support, then don't you bother at all. He may well succeed on his own, but you cannot claim any benefit, role, or joy in his success. Yet ministering to, and serving, others is what it has been about from the First Century until today.

**Urge the New Person at Once
to Seek the Help of the Creator, Our God**

Ignore, and tell the new person to ignore, those who tell him not to study the Bible or anything but the A.A. Big Book. Ignore, and tell the new person to ignore, those who tell him to get a higher power that can be the group, Somebody, Something, or whatever he wants "it" to be. Ignore, and tell the new person to ignore, those who tell him to put his Heavenly Father, his Bible, his religion, and his church second to his sobriety. This kind of nonsense has caused an immense intrusion into the real spirituality (reliance on the Creator) of early A.A. Point out to the new man the history of A.A. It was a Christian fellowship. It studied the Bible. It held frequent prayer meetings. Individual members read Christian literature. Individuals and groups observed "Quiet Times" in and out of meetings, in and out of homes, and in and out of the presence of others. Ignore, and tell the new person to ignore, those who ridicule, criticize, or try to discourage reliance on the Creator, or Bible study, or church, or prayer. Know your A.A. history. Know what our founders actually said about these things in the moments of greatest success. Know your Bible. Know your God. And go tell! Go tell it on the mountain, as the old hymn said.

**Confirm First Your New Person's Belief in God,
His Son, and the Bible**

"Surrenders" were a must in early A.A. They were required as soon as possible—in the hospital or in the first meeting. They meant coming to God through acceptance of Jesus Christ as Lord and Saviour. The status of being or becoming one of God's kids through a new birth was paramount. It occurred first. Bible study was paramount also. So was prayer. So was seeking God's guidance. So were seeking God's love, mercy, grace, forgiveness, healing, and deliverance. Without these, the new person simply spins his wheels in a secular sphere—not marching toward recovery and cure in a spiritual pursuit.

Learn, Understand, Teach, and Support the A.A. Program Itself

Nothing seems more useless than to force or push people into A.A. without understanding what A.A. was and is. To put people in a bus or give them a card and tell them to "attend" gives little impetus to the need for God, for the Bible, for Jesus Christ, for spiritual growth, and for fellowship with God Almighty. To talk about a "higher power," a "spiritual program," "going to meetings," and "outside issues" leaves the prospect in a hopeless pit of confusion. If you do not know the contents of the A.A. Big Book, well, then learn them! If you do not know that the Twelve Steps are the heart of the recovery program, then learn that fact. If you do not know the order and purpose and method of the Twelve Steps, then learn them. The Big Book has hundreds of practical suggestions. The Twelve Steps have some important principles for changing one's life for the better. The meetings are probably the least important facet of Alcoholics Anonymous, but have become almost the subject of doctrine. If you do not go to meetings, you drink, they say. And that is absurd. If you do not want to quit, if you will not seek God's help, if you will not adopt the life-changing principles of the Bible and the Big Book, if you will not develop a spiritual life, if you will not help others to do likewise, then you are not involving yourself in the A.A. program of yesteryear. You also may well become one of those who make up today's 75% to 93% *failure rate*.

If someone bleeding deacon wants to challenge your linking A.A. to God and the Bible, that person—often an angry trouble-maker—is free to drink his relief from a bottle; go to another meeting or group or fellowship; try some inanimate "god" of his own manufacture; or embrace another religion, another program, or another treatment method. A.A. has a program. Originally, it was based exclusively on the power of God. Its Big Book still retains that kind of emphasis; and that should be the heart of your participation and recommendations if your are in the A.A. scene. You are not required to toss out God or the Bible or Jesus Christ. You do have to stand your ground and resist the fiery darts. Alcoholism and addiction are life and death matters. So is seeking God's help a life and death matter.

There is more at work in A.A. to defeat you than the temptation of liquor. The Tempter himself never gives up on his program to defeat the believer. See John 10:10; 2 Peter 5:8-9; James 4:7. And Jesus Christ handled temptations beautifully and effectively when he simply told the devil what the Word of God said (i.e., "It is written"), contrary to what the devil was saying. Luke, Chapter 4, states God's formula for defeating the Tempter. Each time the devil offered Jesus an earthly counterfeit—food, the kingdoms of the world, worship of the devil, and tempting God himself, Jesus responded by quoting and standing on rightly divided Scripture, saying "It is written." (See Luke 4:1-12). Seeing himself ignored and spurned by the truths in the Word of God, the devil took off—for a while. Luke 4:13 states: "And when the devil had ended all the temptation, he departed from him [Jesus] for a season." To understand that the battle against temptation will last as long as the devil lasts is not rejection of cure; it is understanding the nature and tactics of the enemy.

As Dr. Carl Jung suggested to Bill Wilson many years after A.A. was founded, there is a spiritual battle. *"Spirtus contra spiritum,"* wrote Dr. Jung. And see Ephesians, Chapter 6. If drinking could be defeated by just not drinking, there would certainly be no call for an Alcoholics Anonymous Fellowship. If the devil's temptations could be defeated by willpower alone, there would be no need for God's help. But—for those who understand and want to win the spiritual battle—there is need to "Put on the whole armour of God, that ye may be able to stand against the wiles of the devil" (Ephesians 6:11). Ephesians 6:10 declares part of the believer's task: "Finally, my brethren, be strong in the Lord, and in the power of his might." Those in early A.A. saw the need for gaining strength from God and from the power of His might. And you can help the new person by showing from the Word of God that the strength and the power are available today, as yesterday, and as in the days that Paul wrote of them to the Ephesians.

Teach the New Person to Guard and Focus His Tongue

Throughout Oxford Group literature, the writings of Sam Shoemaker, the language of the devotionals, the contents of Anne Smith's journal, and the talks by Dr. Bob, you will see references to the Book of James and winning the battle against the loose and harmful tongue. These are some of the verses:

> And the tongue is a fire, a world of iniquity: so is the tongue among our members, that it defileth the whole body, and setteth on fire the course of nature; and it is set on fire of hell. For every kind of beasts, and of birds, and of serpents, and of things in the sea, is tamed, and hath been tamed of mankind: But the tongue can no man tame; it is an unruly evil, full of deadly poison. Therewith bless we God, even the Father; and therewith curse we men, which are made after the similitude of God. Out of the same mouth proceedeth blessing and cursing. My brethren, these things ought not so to be (James 3:6-10)

Part of what you can tell the new person is not just that his *behavior* needs to be focused on doing the will of God. So must what comes out of his mouth. Psalm 34:13 admonishes: "Keep thy tongue from evil, and thy lips from speaking guile." Psalm 71:8 petitions: "Let my mouth be filled *with* thy praise *and with* thy honour all the day." Proverbs 5:16-19 proclaims: "These six *things* doth the Lord hate: yea, seven are an abomination unto him: A proud look, a lying tongue, and hands that shed innocent blood, An heart that deviseth wicked imaginations, feet that be swift in running to mischief. A false witness *that* speaketh lies, and he that soweth discord among brethren." Note: "An angry man stirreth up strife, and a furious man aboundeth in transgression" (Proverbs 29:22). Contrast Philippians 4:8: "Finally, brethren, whatsoever things are true, whatsoever things *are* honest, whatsoever things *are* just, whatsoever things *are* pure, whatsoever things *are* lovely, whatsoever things *are* of good report; if *there be* any virtue, and if *there be* any praise, think on these things." Finally: "For this cause also thank we God without ceasing, because, when ye received of us the word of God, which ye heard of us, ye received *it* not *as* the word of men, but as it is in truth the word of God, which effectually worketh also in you that believe" (1 Thessalonians 2:13). And when AAs ask what the will of God is, that will can be found in His word in such verses as quoted above. The mind, the mouth, and the deed are all to be set on what God says (Colossians 3). The mouth is not to confess fear, defeat, sickness, anger, envy, anxiety, and a hundred other negatives that are contrary to the truths in the Good Book. When the new person mouths the negatives, he thereby spurns and turns away from the power of God and the truths of His Word, by the freedom of his own speech. What he confesses, he believes; and what he believes can bless him or defeat him depending on whether it is or is not in accordance with

God's will God states the proper attitude toward action and speech: "And whatsoever ye do in word or deed, do all in the name of the Lord Jesus, giving thanks to God and the Father by him" (Colossians 3:17).

Teach Him to Guard and Focus His Thoughts As Well

Still more is required. What you do and what you say need to be consistent with God's commandments. *So do the thoughts you put in your mind and hold in your mind*:

> If there be therefore any consolation in Christ, if any comfort of love, if any fellowship of the Spirit, if any bowels and mercies, Fulfil ye my joy, that ye be like-minded, having the same love, being of one accord, of one mind. Let nothing be done through strife or vainglory; but in lowliness of mind let each esteem other better than themselves. Look not every man on his own things, but every man also on the things of others. Let this mind be in you, which was also in Christ Jesus (Philippians 2:1-5)

> If so be that ye have heard him, and have been taught by him, as the truth is in Jesus: That ye put off concerning the former conversation the old man, which is corrupt according to the deceitful lusts; And be renewed in the spirit of your mind; And that ye put on the new man, which after God is created in righteousness and true holiness (Ephesians 4:21-24).

> Let the word of Christ dwell in you richly in all wisdom; teaching and admonishing one another in psalms and hymns and spiritual songs, singing with grace in your hearts to the Lord (Colossians 3:16).

The new person needs to know that his thoughts, words, and deeds will make a total difference as to the cure he seeks if they are tied to what God tells us to think, say, and do. And the Good Book is filled with instructions to that effect.

Shooting for Long Term Goals

If you look at what Dr. Bob was saying and teaching in the early meetings, you'll see he was seldom talking about alcohol or abstinence. He was talking about applying the Bible and its teachings

My Own Table of Tips

to everyday life. Incidentally, that was the focus of the Oxford Group and Sam Shoemaker as well. The same is true as to what you will find in Anne Smith's journal. And I have seen that same focus carried forward by Dr. Bob's sponsee Clarence Snyder from the beginning to the end of his long-term sobriety, and in the spiritual retreats he founded and conducted.

The new person is adrift in every sense of the word. He needs help in focusing on what God can do for him in every realm of his life once he quits the self-destructive behavior that accompanied his drunkenness. If you focus on trashing God, the Bible, religion, and church, as well the Oxford Group shortcomings, you are left with little in recovery programs but talk. Talk about sex and "relationships." Talk about anger and fear. Talk about gratitude, unity, service, acceptance, and a host of other subjects that hardly equip the cured alcoholic to go forward with quality, godly life. You do not have to be a psychologist, doctor, nurse, clergyman, or counselor to provide the help, although you could be any of those and do your part on the battlefront.

Here are some of the areas where the cured person needs help and where you can assist him in receiving and obtaining that help. Some are new, and some have already been covered but bear repeating:

Truthful information about God, Jesus Christ, the Bible, the gift of Holy Spirit, and the part these played in early recoveries.

As Dr. Bob did, and as the early meetings did, help the fledgling to make time for God and seek Him at every opportunity and throughout every day. A new life does not end with the new birth. It begins!

The important role of medicine, health, nutrition, exercise, personal hygiene, public hygiene, and physical fitness in a useful, successful lifestyle that serves God and others.

The present-day craze for body building; exercising; sports; supplements; vitamins; diets; good nutrition; proper breathing; overcoming obesity; and preventing alzheimers, high blood pressure, cancer, high cholesterol, diabetes, and all the rest offers a focus of major necessity and importance to the beaten-down body and mind of the alcoholic.

Healthy rest, relaxation, and recreation that offer excellent substitutes for dissipation, isolation, and loneliness.

Much of what the cured person does with his "spare" time makes a difference in whether or not his interests are turned away from self-destructive behavior.

10
Cured and Victorious! Putting the Pieces Together

Yes! The Alcoholic Can Be Cured

The alcoholic and the addict can be cured by the power of God. If you do not believe that, then you need to review the history and statements of the founders of A.A. They said they were cured. And they were so convinced of the fact that they devoted their lives to passing on that truth.

Once a Leper, Always a Leper?

Amidst all the talk by A.A.'s three first members that they had been cured, Bill Wilson chose—four years later—to put three sentences in his Big Book that purported to negate his own cure and that of the pioneers. Three sentences! After four years of victories. Those sentences (and that is a good word—*sentences, sentences to be returned to bondage*) are still with us today. The first sentence was: "We have seen the truth demonstrated again and again: 'Once an alcoholic, always an alcoholic'." (*Alcoholics Anonymous*, 4th ed., p. 33). The other two sentences were: "We are not cured of alcoholism. What we really have is a daily reprieve contingent on the maintenance of our spiritual condition" (*Alcoholics Anonymous*, 4th ed., p. 85). Bill cites no medical authority that documents these three sentences. To be sure, Jellinek's "disease concept" fits nicely with Bill's theory [E. M. Jellinek, *The Disease Concept of Alcoholism* (New Haven: CT: College and University Press, 1960)]; yet there is no definitive proof that alcoholics do not quit for good or that they cannot drink again with impunity. [See, for example, Herbert Fingarette. *Heavy Drinking: The Myth of Alcoholism as a Disease* (Berkeley, CA: University of California Press, 1988); Stanton Peele. *Diseasing of America: Addiction Treatment Out of Control* (San Francisco, CA: Jossey Bass, 1995).] Bill cited no religious authority for the three sentences; yet those three propositions are vital as supports for Bill's perpetual sickness with daily reprieve theories. None of the sentences squares with Dr. Bob's views, as I read them.

Consider, please, whether the following are—as they sure seem to be—complete absurdities. Suppose, just for ducks, you decide to revise the Bible and its descriptions of the healings of Jesus. First, would you want to? Second, on what authority? And third, just look at the absurd results:

Example 1:

Matthew 4:23-24:
And Jesus went about all Galilee, teaching in their synagogues, and preaching the gospel of the kingdom, and healing all manner of sickness and all manner of disease among the people.
And his fame went throughout all Syria: and they brought unto him all sick people that were taken with divers diseases and torments, and those which were possessed with devils and those which were lunatick, and those that had the palsy; and he healed them.

Absurdity: We got this basic idea from the Bible, but Jesus must surely have warned all these people that they could never be cured and merely had a daily reprieve contingent on the maintenance of their spiritual condition.

Example 2:

Matthew 8:2-3:
And, behold, there came a leper and worshipped him, saying, Lord, if thou wilt, thou canst make me clean.
And Jesus put forth his hand, and touched him, saying, I will; be thou clean. And immediately his leprosy was cleansed.

Absurdity. We got this basic idea from the Bible, but Jesus must have also have told the leper: One day at a time. Don't expect too much.

Cured and Victorious! Putting the Pieces Together   131

Once a leper, always a leper. Just wait. You are eligible too! Relapse is OK. Don't worry about it. You can always go back to "treatment."

Example 3:

Matthew 9:27-30a:
And when Jesus departed thence, two blind men followed him, crying and saying, *Thou* son of David, have mercy on us.
And when he was come into the house, the blind men came to him: and Jesus saith unto them, Believe ye that I am able to do this? They said unto him, Yea, Lord.
Then touched he their eyes, saying, According to your faith be it unto you.
And their eyes were opened. . . ."

Absurdity: We got this basic idea from the Bible, but Jesus must have told the blind men: You are not really cured. Just keep going to meetings. The only fear to keep in mind is the fear that you will go blind again. Acceptance is the answer.

Example 4:

Matthew 11:4-5:
Jesus answered and said unto them, Go and shew John again those things which ye do hear and see:
The blind receive their sight, and the lame walk, the lepers are cleansed, and the deaf hear, the dead are raised up, and the poor have the gospel preached to them.

Absurdity. We got this basic idea from the Bible, but do not give it much credence. Jesus must have added: The blind did not really receive their sight; the lame did not really walk; the lepers are still lepers; the deaf still cannot hear a darned thing; and the dead are not really alive. My miracles have been highly overrated.

I leave to you with our real question: Whether God could and did and can and will cure alcoholics. I leave that question to you, along with the language of Bill Wilson, Bob Smith, and Bill Dotson that *they were cured.* I leave it to you with Bill's repeated statement that *they were "recovered."* I leave it to you with Bill's insistent statement: "*And it means, of course, that we are going to talk about*

God" (*Alcoholics Anonymous*, 4th ed., p. 45). I believe I could make a pretty strong case to a jury that alcoholics were cured and could be cured until their followers were introduced to other gods, to higher powers, to radiators and light bulbs, and to Somebodies and Somethings. That is when the A.A. ratings slipped, I'd argue. And I do! God rates high on the cure scale. Radiators are below three percent--something like zero.

Far More Than Cure Awaits God's Kids

There is more. If you seek the kingdom of God and His righteousness, you'll get more than a cure. Here is some of it.

". . . I [Jesus] am come that they might have life, and that they might have *it* more abundantly"

You are one of God's kids. You have got Jesus's assurance that he came to make available life and that you might have it more abundantly (John 10:10). His Father delivered you from the power of darkness (Colossians 1:13). You have got the promise that perfect love—the love of God—casts out fear (1 John 4:18). You have got the assurance of God's will that, above all things, you prosper and be in health (3 John 2). Your peace rests on what Jesus Christ did for you: "Who his own self bare our sins in his own body on the tree, that, we, being dead to sins, should live unto righteousness: by whose stripes ye were healed" (1 Peter 2:24). That is for those of us still alive.

My life really changed in sobriety as I learned more and more how much God loves me, and how much he has made available to me.

". . . That whosoever believeth in him [God's Son, Jesus] should not perish, but have everlasting life"

There is more, by far. There is the gathering together of believers when Jesus Christ returns. Here's just a piece of that picture:

> For God so loved the world, that he gave his only begotten Son, that whosoever believeth in him should not perish, but have everlasting life (John 3:16).

He that believeth on the Son hath everlasting life: and he that believeth not the Son shall not see life; but the wrath of God abideth on him (John 3:36).

And [Jesus] said unto them, Thus it is written, and thus it behoved Christ to suffer, and to rise from the dead the third day: And that repentance and remission of sins should be preached in his name among all nations, beginning at Jerusalem. And ye are witnesses of these things. And, behold, I send the promise of my Father upon you: but tarry ye in the city of Jerusalem, until ye be endued with power from on high (Luke 24:46-49).

And while they looked stedfastly toward heaven as he [Jesus] went up, behold, two men stood by them in white apparel; Which also said, Ye men of Galilee, why stand ye gazing up into heaven? This same Jesus, which is taken up from you into heaven, shall so come in like manner as ye have seen him go into heaven (Acts 1:10-11).

If in this life only we have hope in Christ, we are of all men most miserable. But now is Christ risen from the dead, and become the firstfruits of them that slept. For since by man came death, by man came also the resurrection of the dead. For as in Adam all die, even so in Christ shall all be made alive. But every man in his own order: Christ the firstfruits; afterward they that are Christ's at his coming (1 Corinthians 15:19-23).

Behold, I shew you a mystery: We shall not all sleep, but we shall all be changed. For this corruptible must put on incorruption, and this mortal must put on immortality. So when this corruptible shall have put on incorruption, and this mortal shall have put on immortality, then shall be brought to pass the saying that is written, Death is swallowed up in victory (1 Corinthians 15:51-54).

For they themselves shew of us what manner of entering in we had unto you, and how ye turned to God from idols to serve the living and true God; And to wait for his Son from heaven, whom he raised from the dead, even Jesus, which delivered us from the wrath to come (1 Thessalonians 1:9-10).

For God hath not appointed us to wrath, but to obtain salvation by our Lord Jesus Christ. Who died for us, that, whether we wake or sleep, we should live together with him (1 Thessalonians 5:9-10).

Now we beseech you, brethren, by the coming of our Lord Jesus Christ, and by our gathering together unto him, That ye be not soon shaken in mind, or be troubled, neither by spirit, nor by word, nor by letter as from us, as that day of Christ is at hand (2 Thessalonians 2:1-2).

This Bible Stuff Need Not Drive Anyone up a Tree

It seems strange what historians are doing with our history. One has described any book that talks about the Bible and A.A. as lacking in integrity and just plain "preaching." As if preaching were some sin. Where do such angry denunciations come from? Another historian has called my research and the unearthing of our history my "hobby." As if putting a diminutive label on careful research will somehow reduce its recognition and importance. Some, who are not historians, get off on the side spur that anything that talks about the Bible or Christ within A.A. violates the Twelve Traditions. As if A.A. somehow passed a law that the Bible has now been banned. Some say any return of enthusiasm for A.A.'s roots is designed to exclude all but Christians from Alcoholics Anonymous. Says who! As if we should somehow ignore the fact that A.A. right now has over two million "members" who hold a wide variety of faiths and that many have no faith at all and often say so. Some obfuscate by saying A.A. is not religious, but spiritual. What in the world does that nonsensical expression mean? As if they have some way of explaining the supposed difference between religious and spiritual when the Pope has declared that "spirituality" is establishing a relationship with Jesus Christ, and court after court today is ruling that A.A. is a religion. Some say we do not need history. What nonsense in view of the proliferation of archivists and archives conferences in A.A. As if a knowledge of that history might endanger our species. Some do not want this particular part of our history. "Just the spiritual part," they say. As if you can take half of God, half of the Bible, half of religion, and half of a slice of baloney, digest it, and smile while still trying to understand the "God part"—which is really the entirety of A.A.'s heart. "God" still stands out like a diamond amidst the proliferation of "higher powers" in present-day thinking.

But none of that really matters at all.

It Is about Victory

In the beginning, pioneer A.A. offered victory. You can see that victory in the various books they studied on the "life of Jesus Christ."You can see it in the variety and diversity of books they read on and about Jesus's "Sermon on the Mount" [See Dick B., *The Books Early AAs Read for Spiritual Growth*, 7th ed. (Kihei: HI: Paradise Research Publications, 1998).]You can see that victory in the title AAs originally wanted to use for their basic text—"The Way Out." You can see it in Dr. Bob's concluding statement in his personal story: "Your Heavenly Father will never let you down!" (Big Book, 4th ed., p. 181). The victory does not involve prescriptions for everlasting illness. The victory means assured victory over alcoholism and all its attendant problems, victory—based on the Bible:

> Now thanks *be* unto God, which always causeth us to triumph in Christ, and maketh manifest the savour of his knowledge by us in every place (2 Corinthians 2:14)

> But thanks *be* to God, which giveth us the victory through our Lord Jesus Christ. Therefore, my beloved brethren, be ye stedfast, unmoveable, always abounding in the work of the Lord, forasmuch as ye know that your labour is not in vain in the Lord (1 Corinthians 15:57, 58).

> For whosoever is born of God overcometh the world: and this is the victory that overcometh the world, *even* our faith. Who is he that overcometh the world, but he that believeth that Jesus is the Son of God (1 John 5:4-5).

If you'd like to confirm for yourself that these verses on triumph were those, among others, early AAs were reading, take a good hard look at the four years of *The Upper Room* quarterlies, for the years 1935 to 1939, that the pioneers used in their daily devotionals. Read the other books early AAs read and which are listed and discussed in Dick B., *Dr. Bob and His Library*. 3rd ed. (Kihei: HI: Paradise Research Publications, 1998); *Anne Smith's Journal, 1933-1939.* 3rd

ed. (Kihei, HI: Paradise Research Publications, 1998); and *The Books Early AAs Read for Spiritual Growth*, 7th ed. (Kihei, HI: Paradise Research Publications, 1998).

It Is about God's Love

If it were necessary (and it is not), I'd go to the mat with anyone who says it is wrong to tell someone in Alcoholics Anonymous that God loves them, that God is love, or that "Thy will be done" (as a statement that the commandments of God are to be done) represents the love of God. Bill Wilson, Dr. Bob Smith, and Anne Smith, Bob's wife, said those things over and over again.

I have published eighteen titles that document the facts stated here. And I published eighteen titles that document the fact that, if you took every verse in the Bible from all my eighteen books, you would be removing only a part of what early AAs and their families read and believed in the Good Book.

Telling it like it *was* does not mean you have to want it like it was, or is. However, I shudder to think what America would look like today if we hadn't preserved, studied, and applied the principles in the Declaration of Independence, the United States Constitution, and the Bill of Rights. I am thankful to God that we have still been able to find and speak about our A.A. history. I am thankful to God that we have our cures. I am thankful to say that he who turns to God for cure, for the abundant life, and for an everlasting life can and will find them all—whether in or out of A.A. And I hope you can help him find them in or out of A.A. I am thankful to God, no matter what, because He has done for me what I could not do for myself. To say the least, I am cured! And I am thankful to God for the victory!

End

Bibliography

Alcoholics Anonymous

Publications About

Alcoholics Anonymous. (multilith volume). New Jersey: Works Publishing Co., 1939.
Alcoholics Anonymous: The Story of How More Than 100 Men Have Recovered from Alcoholism. New York City: Works Publishing Company, 1939.
E., Bob. *Handwritten note to Lois Wilson on pamphlet entitled "Four Absolutes."* (copy made available to the author at Founders Day Archives Room in Akron, Ohio, in June, 1991).
———. Letter from Bob E. to Nell Wing. Stepping Stones Archives.
B., Dick. *Anne Smith's Journal, 1933-1939: A.A.'s Principles of Success.* 3rd ed. Kihei, HI: Paradise Research Publications, 1998.
———. *The Oxford Group & Alcoholics Anonymous: A Design for Living That Works.* 3d ed. Kihei, HI: Paradise Research Publications, 1998.
———. *Dr. Bob and His Library: A Major A.A. Spiritual Source.* 3rd ed. Kihei, HI: Paradise Research Publications, 1998.
———. *New Light on Alcoholism: God, Sam Shoemaker, and A.A.,* 2d ed.. Kihei, HI: Paradise Research Publications, 1999.
———. *That Amazing Grace: The Role of Clarence and Grace S. in Alcoholics Anonymous.* San Rafael, CA: Paradise Research Publications, 1996.
———. *The Akron Genesis of Alcoholics Anonymous.* 3rd ed. Kihei, HI: Paradise Research Publications, 1998.
———. *The Books Early AAs Read for Spiritual Growth.* 7th ed., Kihei, HI, CA: Paradise Research Publications, 1998.
———. *The Good Book and The Big Book: A.A.'s Roots in the Bible.* 2d ed., Kihei, HI: Paradise Research Publications, 1997.
———, and Bill Pittman. *Courage to Change: The Christian Roots of the 12-Step Movement.* Grand Rapids, MI: Fleming H. Revell, 1994.
———. *Turning Point: A History of Early A.A.'s Spiritual Roots and Successes.* Kihei, HI: Paradise Research Publications, 1997.
———. *Good Morning! Quiet Time, Morning Watch, Meditation, and Early A.A..* 2d ed. Kihei, HI: Paradise Research Publications, 1998.
———. *Utilizing Early A.A.'s Spiritual Roots for Recovery Today.* Kihei, HI: Paradise Research Publications, 1998.
———. *The Golden Text of A.A.: Early A.A., God, and Real Spirituality.* Kihei, HI: Paradise Research Publications, 1999.
———. *By the Power of God: A Guide to Early A.A. Groups & Forming Similar Groups Today.* Kihei, HI: Paradise Research Publications, 2000.
———. *Making Known the Biblical History and Roots of Alcoholics Anonymous.* Kihei, HI: Paradise Research Publications, 2001.
———. *Why Early A.A. Succeeded: The Good Book in A.A. Yesterday and Today.* Kihei, HI: Paradise Research Publications, 2001.
———. *Hope! The Story of Geraldine Delaney, Alina Lodge, & Recovery.* 2d ed, Kihei, HI: Tincture of Time Press, 2002.
———. *God and Alcoholism: Our Growing Opportunity in the 21st Century.* Kihei, HI: Paradise Research Publications, Inc., 2002.

B., Jim. *Evolution of Alcoholics Anonymous.* New York: A.A. Archives.
C., Stewart. *A Reference Guide to the Big Book of Alcoholics Anonymous.* Seattle: Recovery Press, 1986.
Clapp, Charles, Jr. *Drinking's Not the Problem.* New York: Thomas Y. Crowell, 1949.
Darrah, Mary C. *Sister Ignatia: Angel of Alcoholics Anonymous.* Chicago: Loyola University Press, 1992.
Fitzgerald, Robert. *The Soul of Sponsorship: The Friendship of Father Ed Dowling, S.J., and Bill Wilson in Letters.* Center City, Minn.: Hazelden, 1995.
Hunter, Willard, with assistance from M. D. B. *A.A.'s Roots in the Oxford Group.* New York: A.A. Archives, 1988.
Knippel, Charles T. *Samuel M. Shoemaker's Theological Influence on William G. Wilson's Twelve Step Spiritual Program of Recovery.* Ph. D. dissertation. St. Louis University, 1987.
Kurtz, Ernest. *Not-God: A History of Alcoholics Anonymous.* Exp. ed. Minnesota: Hazelden, 1991.
Morreim, Dennis C. *Changed Lives: The Story of Alcoholics Anonymous.* Minneapolis: Augsburg Fortress, 1991.
Morse, Robert M, M.D., and Daniel K. Flavin, M.D. "The Definition of Alcoholism." *The Journal of the American Medical Association.* August 26, 1992, pp. 1012-14.
P., Wally. *But, for the Grace of God . . .: How Intergroups & Central Offices Carried the Message of Alcoholics Anonymous in the 1940s.* West Virginia: The Bishop of Books, 1995.
Pittman, Bill. *AA The Way It Began.* Seattle: Glen Abbey Books, 1988.
Poe, Stephen E. and Frances E. *A Concordance to Alcoholics Anonymous.* Nevada: Purple Salamander Press, 1990.
Robertson, Nan. *Getting Better Inside Alcoholics Anonymous.* New York: William Morrow & Co., 1988.
S., Clarence. *Going through the Steps.* 2d ed. Altamonte Springs, FL: Stephen Foreman, 1985.
———. *My Higher Power—The Lightbulb.* 2d ed. Altamonte Springs, FL: Stephen Foreman, 1985.
Seiberling, John F. *Origins of Alcoholics Anonymous.* (A transcript of remarks by Henrietta B. Seiberling: transcript prepared by Congressman John F. Seiberling of a telephone conversation with his mother, Henrietta in the spring of 1971): Employee Assistance Quarterly. 1985; (1); pp. 8-12.
Smith, Bob and Sue Smith Windows. *Children of the Healer.* Illinois: Parkside Publishing Corporation, 1992.
Thomsen, Robert. *Bill W.* New York: Harper & Row, 1975.
Walker, Richmond. *For Drunks Only.* Minnesota: Hazelden, n.d.
———. *The 7 Points of Alcoholics Anonymous.* Seattle: Glen Abbey Books, 1989.
Wilson, Bill. *How The Big Book Was Put Together.* New York: A.A. General Services Archives, Transcript of Bill Wilson Speech delivered in Fort Worth, Texas, 1954.
———. *Bill Wilson's Original Story.* Bedford Hills, New York: Stepping Stones Archives, n.d., a manuscript whose individual lines are numbered 1 to 1180.
———. "Main Events: Alcoholics Anonymous Fact Sheet by Bill." November 1, 1954. Stepping Stones Archives. Bedford Hills, New York.
———. "The Fellowship of Alcoholics Anonymous." *Quarterly Journal of Studies on Alcohol.* Yale University, 1945, pp. 461-73.
———. *W. G. Wilson Recollections.* Bedford Hills, New York: Stepping Stones Archives, September 1, 1954 transcript of Bill's dictations to Ed B.
Wilson, Jan R., and Judith A. Wilson. *Addictionary: A Primer of Recovery Terms and Concepts from Abstinence to Withdrawal.* New York: Simon and Schuster, 1992.
Wilson, Lois. *Lois Remembers.* New York: Al-Anon Family Group Headquarters, 1987.

Bibliography 139

Windows, Sue Smith. (daughter of A.A.'s Co-Founder, Dr. Bob). Typewritten Memorandum entitled, *Henrietta and early Oxford Group Friends, by Sue Smith Windows*. Delivered to the author of this book by Sue Smith Windows at Akron, June, 1991.

Wing, Nell. *Grateful to Have Been There: My 42 Years with Bill and Lois, and the Evolution of Alcoholics Anonymous*. Illinois: Parkside Publishing Corporation, 1992.

Publications Approved by Alcoholics Anonymous

Alcoholics Anonymous. 4th ed. New York: Alcoholics Anonymous World Services, 2001
Alcoholics Anonymous. 3rd ed. New York: Alcoholics Anonymous World Services, 1976.
Alcoholics Anonymous. 1st ed. New Jersey: Works Publishing, 1939.
Alcoholics Anonymous Comes of Age. New York: Alcoholics Anonymous World Services, 1957.
A Newcomer Asks . . . York, England: A.A. Sterling Area Services, n.d.
As Bill Sees It: The A.A. Way of Life . . . selected writings of A.A.'s Co-Founder. New York: Alcoholics Anonymous World Services, 1967.
Best of the Grapevine. New York: The A.A. Grapevine, Inc., 1985.
Best of the Grapevine, Volume II. New York: The A.A. Grapevine, Inc., 1986.
Came to Believe. New York: Alcoholics Anonymous World Services, 1973.
Daily Reflections. New York: Alcoholics Anonymous World Services, 1991.
DR. BOB and the Good Oldtimers. New York: Alcoholics Anonymous World Services, 1980.
44 Questions. New York: Works Publishing, Inc., 1952.
Members of the Clergy Ask about Alcoholics Anonymous. New York: Alcoholics Anonymous World Services, 1961, 1979-revised 1992, according to 1989 Conference Advisory Action.
Pass It On. New York: Alcoholics Anonymous World Services, 1984.
Questions & Answers on Sponsorship. New York: Alcoholics Anonymous World Services, 1976.
The A.A. Grapevine: "RHS"—issue dedicated to the memory of the Co-Founder of Alcoholics Anonymous, DR. BOB. New York: A.A. Grapevine, Inc., 1951.
The A.A. Service Manual. New York: Alcoholics Anonymous World Services, 1990-1991.
The Co-Founders of Alcoholics Anonymous. New York: Alcoholics Anonymous World Services, 1972.
The Language of the Heart. Bill W.'s Grapevine Writings. New York: The A.A. Grapevine, Inc., 1988.
This is A.A. . . . An Introduction to the A.A. Recovery Program. New York: Alcoholics Anonymous World Services, 1984.
Twelve Steps and Twelve Traditions. New York: Alcoholics Anonymous World Services, 1953.

Pamphlets Circulated in Early A.A.

A. A. Sponsorship: Its Opportunities and Its Responsibilities. Cleveland: Cleveland Ohio District Office, 1944.
A Guide to the Twelve Steps of Alcoholics Anonymous. Akron: AA of Akron, n.d.
Alcoholics Anonymous: An Interpretation of our Twelve Steps. Washington, D.C.: Paragon Creative Printers, 1944.
A Manual for Alcoholics Anonymous. Akron: AA of Akron, n.d.
Central Bulletin, Volumes I - III. Cleveland Central Committee, October, 1942 - December, 1945.
"It's All in the Mind" Chicago: Chicago Area Alcoholics Anonymous Service Office, n.d.

Second Reader for Alcoholics Anonymous. Akron: AA of Akron, n.d.
Spiritual Milestones in Alcoholics Anonymous. Akron: A.A. of Akron, n.d.
The New Way of Life: A.A. Cleveland: The Cleveland District Office of Alcoholics Anonymous, n.d.
T., John. *A.A.: God's Instrument*. Chicago: Chicago Area Alcoholics Anonymous Service Office, n.d.
The Four Absolutes. Cleveland: Cleveland Central Committee of A.A., n.d.
Twelve Steps of AA and The Bible. From the collection of Clancy U., n.d.
What Others Think of A.A. Akron: Friday Forum Luncheon Club, circa 1941.

Alcoholics Anonymous: Pro, Con, and Evaluated

A Program for You: A Guide to the Big Book's Design for Living. Hazelden Foundation, 1991.
B., Mel. *New Wine: The Spiritual Roots of the Twelve Step Miracle*. Hazelden Foundation, 1991.
Baker, John. *Celebrate Recovery*. Lake Forest, CA: Celebrate Recovery Books, 1994.
Bartosch, Bob and Pauline. *A Bridge to Recovery*. La Habra, CA: Overcomers Outreach, Inc., 1994.
Bobgan, Martin and Deidre. *12 Steps to Destruction: Codependency Recovery Heresies*. Santa Barbara, CA: EastGate Publishers, 1991.
Bufe, Charles. *Alcoholics Anonymous: Cult or Cure?* 2d ed. AZ: Sharp Press, 1998.
Burns, Dr. Cathy. *Alcoholics Anonymous Unmasked: Deception and Deliverance*. Mt. Carmel, PA: Sharing, 1991.
Catanzaro, Ronald J. *Alcoholism: The Total Treatment Approach*. IL: Charles C. Thomas Publisher, 1968.
Chafetz, Morris E., and Harold W. Demone, Jr. *Alcoholism and Society*. New York: Oxford University Press, 1962.
Chambers, Cal. *Two Tracks-One Goal: How Alcoholics Anonymous Relates to Christianity*. Langley, B.C., Canada: Credo Publishing Corporation, 1992.
Clinebell, Howard. *Understanding and Counseling Persons with Alcohol, Drug, and Behavioral Addictions*. Rev. and enl. ed. Nashville: Abingdon Press, 1998.
_____. *Well Being: A Personal Plan for Exploring and Enriching the Seven Dimensions of Life*. NY: HarperSan Francisco, 1992.
Costantino, Frank. *Holes in Time: The Autobiography of a Gangster*. 2d ed. Dallas, TX: Acclaimed Books, 1986.
Cunningham, Loren. *Is That Really You, God?: Hearing the Voice of God*. Seattle, WA: YWAM Publishing, 1984.
Davis, Martin M. *The Gospel and the Twelve Steps: Developing a Closer Relationship with Jesus*. San Diego, CA: Recovery Publications, 1993.
Doyle, Paul Barton. *In Step with God: A Scriptural Guide for Practicing 12 Step Programs*. Brentwood, TN: New Directions, 1989.
Dunn, Jerry G. *God is for the Alcoholic*. Chicago: Moody Press, 1965.
Ellis, Albert, and Emmett Belten. *When A.A. Doesn't Word for You: Rational Steps to Quitting Alcohol*. Fort Lee, NJ: Barricade Books, 1992.
Fingarette, Herbert. *Heavy Drinking: The Myth of Alcoholism as a Disease*. Berkeley, CA: University of California Press, 1988.
Fletcher, Anne M. *Sober for Good: New Solutions for Drinking Problems–Advice from Those Who Have Succeeded*. NY: Houghton Miflin Company, 2001.
Fransway, Rebecca. *12-Step Horror Stories*. Tucson, AZ: See Sharp Press, 2000.
Gilliam, Marianne W. *How Alcoholics Anonymous Failed Me*. NY: Eagle Brook, 1998.
Hemfelt, Robert and Fowler, Richard. *Serenity: A Companion for Twelve Step Recovery*. Nashville, TN: Thomas Nelson Publishers, 1990.

Bibliography

Jellinek, E. M. *The Disease Concept of Alcoholism*. New Haven, CN: College and University Press, 1960.
Johnson, Vernon E. *I'll Quit Tomorrow*. New York: Harper & Row, 1973.
K., Mitchell. *How It Worked: The Story of Clarence H. Snyder and The Early Days of Alcoholics Anonymous in Cleveland, Ohio*. NY: AA Big Book Study Group, 1997.
Kavanaugh, Philip R. *Magnificent Addiction: Discovering Addiction as Gateway to Healing*. Santa Rosa, CA: Asland Publishing, 1992.
Ketcham, Katherine, and William F. Asbury (with Mel Schulstad and Arthur P. Ciaramicoli). *Beyond the Influence: Understanding and Defeating Alcoholism*. New York: Bantam Books, 2000.
Kurtz, Ernest and Ketcham, Katherine. *The Spirituality of Imperfection: Modern Wisdom from Classic Stories*. New York: Bantam Books, 1992.
Landry, Mim J. *Overview of Addiction Treatment Effectiveness*. Rev. ed., 1997. U.S. Department of Health and Human Services.
Larson, Joan Mathews. *Alcoholism–The Biochemical Connection: A Breakthrough Seven-Week Self-Treatment Program*. NY: Villard Books, 1992.
_____. *Seven Weeks to Sobriety: The Proven Program to Fight Alcoholism Through Nutrition*. New York: Fawcett Columbine, 1992
McCrady, Barbara S. and Miller, William R. *Research on Alcoholics Anonymous: Opportunities and* Alternatives. NJ: Publications Division, Rutgers Center of Alcohol Studies, 1993.
May, Gerald G. *Addiction & Grace: Love and Spirituality in the Healing of Addictions*. NY: HarperSanFrancisco, 1988.
McQ., Joe. *The Steps We Took*. Little Rock, AR: August House Publishers, Inc., 1990.
Miller, J. Keith. *A Hunger for Healing: The Twelve Steps as a Classic Model for Christian Spiritual Growth*. San Francisco: HarperSanFrancisco, 1991.
Nace, Edgar P. *The Treatment of Alcoholism*. NY: Brunner/Mazel Publishers, 1987.
O., Dr. Paul. *There's more to Quitting Drinking than Quitting Drinking*. Laguna Niguel, CA: Sabrina Publishing, 1995.
P., Wally. *Back to Basics: The Alcoholics Anonymous Beginners' Classes. Take all 12 Steps in Four One-Hour Sessions*. Tucson, AZ: Faith With Works Publishing Company, 1997.
Paton, Wally. *How to Listen to God: A Guide for Successful Living Through the Practice of Two-way Prayer*. Tucson, AZ: Faith With Works Publishing Company, 2000.
Peale, Norman Vincent. *The Positive Power of Jesus Christ: Life-Changing Adventures in Faith*. Pauling, NY: Foundation for Christian Living, 1980.
_____. *The Power of Positive Thinking*. Pauling, NY: Peale Center for Christian Living, 1978.
Peele, Stanton. *Diseasing of America*. Lexington, MA Lexington Books, 1989.
_____ and Bufe, Charles. *Resisting 12-Step Coercion: How To Fight Forced Participation in AA, NA, or 12-Step Treatment*. Tucson, AZ: See Sharp Press, 2000.
_____. *The Truth About Addiction and Recovery* (with Archie Brodsky). MA: Lexington Books, 1995.
Poley, Wayne and Lea, Gary, and Vibe, Gail. *Alcoholism: A Treatment Manual*. NY: Gardner Press, Inc., 1979.
Playfair, William L. *The Useful Lie*. Wheaton, IL: Crossway Books, 1991.
Ragge, Ken. *More Revealed: A Critical Analysis of Alcoholics Anonymous and the Twelve Steps*. Henderson, NV: Alert! Publishing, 1991.
_____. *The Real AA: Behind the Myth of 12-Step Recovery*. AZ: Sharp Press, 1998.
Rudy, David R. *Becoming Alcoholic: Alcoholics Anonymous and the Reality of Alcoholism*. IL: Southern Illinois University Press, 1986.
Royce, James E. *Alcohol Problems and Alcoholism: A Comprehensive Survey*. NY: The Free Press, 1981.

Life Recovery Bible, The: The Living Bible. Wheaton, IL: Tyndale House Publishers, Inc., 1992.
Salomone, Guy. *Religious and Spiritual Origins of the Twelve Step Recovery Movement*. CA: Lotus Press, 1997.
Seiden, Jerry. *Divine or Distorted?: God As We Understand God*. San Diego, CA: Recovery Publications, 1993.
Selby, Saul. *Twelve Step Christianity: The Christian Roots & Application of the Twelve Steps*. MN: Hazelden, 2000.
Self-Help Sourcebook, The: Your Guide to Community and Online Support Groups. 6th.ed. compiled and edited by Barbara J. White and Edward J. Madara. Denville, NJ: American Self-Help Clearinghouse, 1994.
Spickard, Anderson and Thompson, Barbara R. *Dying for a Drink: What You Should Know about Alcoholism*. Waco, TX: Word Books Publisher, 1985.
Stafford, Tim. *The Hidden Gospel of the 12 Steps*. Christianity Today, July 22, 1991.
Trimpey, Jack. *Rational Recovery: The New Cure for Substance Addiction*. New York: Pocket Books, 1996.
———. *Revolutionary Alternative for Overcoming Alcohol and Drug Dependence, A: The Small Book*. Rev. ed. NY: Delacorte Press, 1992.
U.S. Department of Health and Human Services. Substance Abuse and Mental Health Services Administration. *National Household Survey on Drug Abuse: Main Findings 1996*. Rockville, MD: SAMHSA, Office of Applied Studies, 1998.
Vaillant, George E. *The Natural History of Alcoholism Revisited*. Cambridge, MA: Harvard University Press, 1995.
Van Impe, Jack and Campbell, Roger F. *Alcohol: The Beloved Enemy*. Nashville: Thomas Nelson Publishers, 1980.
Vaughan, Clark. *Addictive Thinking: The Road to Recovery for Problem Drinkers and Those Who Love Them*. NY: The Viking Press, 1982.
Wallis, Jim. *Faith Works. Lessons from the Life of an Activist Preacher*. NY: Random House, 2000.
Washton, Arnold and Boundy, Donna. *Willpower's Not Enough: Understanding and Recovering from Addictions of Every Kind*. NY: Harper & Row Publishers, 1989.
Way Home, The: A Spiritual Approach to Recovery. Orlando, FL: Bridge Builders, Inc., 1996.
White, William L. *Slaying The Dragon: The History of Addiction Treatment and Recovery in America*. Bloomington, IL: Chestnut Health Systems/Lighthouse Institute, 1998
Wing, Nell. *Grateful to have Been There: My 42 Years with Bill and Lois and the Evolution of Alcoholics Anonymous*. Park Ridge, IL: Parkside Publishing Corporation, 1992.

The Bible—Versions of and Books About

Authorized King James Version. New York: Thomas Nelson, 1984.
Bullinger, Ethelbert W. *A Critical Lexicon and Concordance to the English and Greek New Testament*. Michigan: Zondervan, 1981.
Burns, Kenneth Charles. "The Rhetoric of Christology." Master's thesis, San Francisco State University, 1991.
Every Catholic's Guide to the Sacred Scriptures. Nashville: Thomas Nelson, 1990.
Harnack, Adolph. *The Expansion of Christianity in the First Three Centuries*. New York: G. P. Putnam's Sons, Volume I, 1904; Volume II, 1905.
Kohlenberger, John R., III, gen. ed. *The Contemporary Parallel New Testament*. New York: Oxford University Press, 1997.
Megivern, James J. *Official Catholic Teachings: Bible Interpretation*. North Carolina: McGrath Publishing Company, 1978.

Bibliography

Moffatt, James. *A New Translation of the Bible*. New York: Harper & Brothers, 1954.
New Bible Dictionary. 2d ed. Wheaton, Illinois: Tyndale House Publishers, 1987.
Puskas, Charles B. *An Introduction to the New Testament*. Mass.: Hendrickson Publishers, 1989.
Recovery Devotional Bible. Grand Rapids, MI: Zondervan Publishing House, 1993.
Revised Standard Version. New York: Thomas Nelson, 1952.
Serenity: A Companion for Twelve Step Recovery. Nashville: Thomas Nelson, 1990.
Schaff, Philip. *History of the Christian Church*. Grand Rapids, MI: Wm. B. Eerdmans, Volume II, 1956.
Strong, James. *The Exhaustive Concordance of the Bible*. Iowa: Riverside Book and Bible House, n.d.
The Abingdon Bible Commentary. New York: Abingdon Press, 1929.
The Companion Bible. Michigan: Zondervan Bible Publishers, 1964.
The Life Recovery Bible. Wheaton, IL: Tyndale House Publishers, 1992.
The Revised English Bible. Oxford: Oxford University Press, 1989.
Vine, W. E. *Vine's Expository Dictionary of Old and New Testament Words*. New York: Fleming H. Revell, 1981.
Young's Analytical Concordance to the Bible. New York: Thomas Nelson, 1982.
Zodhiates, Spiros. *The Hebrew-Greek Key Study Bible*. 6th ed. AMG Publishers, 1991.

Bible Devotionals

Chambers, Oswald. *My Utmost for His Highest*. London: Simpkin Marshall, Ltd., 1927.
Clark, Glenn, *I Will Lift Up Mine Eyes*. New York: Harper & Brothers, 1937.
Dunnington, Lewis L. *Handles of Power*. New York: Abingdon-Cokesbury Press, 1942.
Fosdick, Harry Emerson. *The Meaning of Prayer*. New York: Association Press, 1915.
Holm, Nora Smith. *The Runner's Bible*. New York: Houghton Mifflin Company, 1915.
Jones, E. Stanley. *Abundant Living*. New York: Abingdon-Cokesbury Press, 1942.
———. *Victorious Living*. New York: Abingdon Press, 1936.
Prescott, D. M. *A New Day: Daily Readings for Our Time*. New ed. London: Grosvenor Books, 1979.
The Upper Room: Daily Devotions for Family and Individual Use. Quarterly. 1st issue: April, May, June, 1935. Edited by Grover Carlton Emmons. Nashville: General Committee on Evangelism through the Department of Home Missions, Evangelism, Hospitals, Board of Missions, Methodist Episcopal Church, South.
Tileston, Mary W. *Daily Strength for Daily Needs*. Boston: Roberts Brothers, 1893.

Publications by or about the Oxford Group & Oxford Group People

A Day in Pennsylvania Honoring Frank Nathan Daniel Buchman in Pennsburg and Allentown. Oregon: Grosvenor Books, 1992.
Allen, Geoffrey Francis. *He That Cometh*. New York: The Macmillan Company, 1933.
Almond, Harry J. *Foundations for Faith*. 2d ed. London: Grosvenor Books, 1980.
———. *Iraqi Statesman: A Portrait of Mohammed Fadhel Jamali*. Salem, OR: Grosvenor Books, 1993.
Austin, H. W. "Bunny". *Frank Buchman As I Knew Him*. London: Grosvenor Books, 1975.
———. *Moral Re-Armament: The Battle for Peace*. London: William Heinemann, 1938.
Batterson, John E. *How to Listen to God*. N.p., n.d.
Bayless, W. N. *The Oxford Group: A Way of Life*, n.d.
Becker, Mrs. George. "Quiet Time in the Home." N.p., n.d.

Begbie, Harold. *Life Changers*. New York: G. P. Putnam's Sons, 1927.
———. *Souls in Action*. New York: Hodder & Stoughton, 1911.
———. *Twice-Born Men*. New York: Fleming H. Revell, 1909.
Belden, David C. *The Origins and Development of the Oxford Group (Moral Re-Armament)*. D. Phil. Dissertation, Oxford University, 1976.
Belden, Kenneth D. *Beyond The Satellites: Is God is Speaking-Are We Listening?* London: Grosvenor Books, 1987.
———. *Meeting Moral Re-Armament*. London: Grosvenor Books, 1979.
———. *Reflections on Moral Re-Armament*. London: Grosvenor Books, 1983.
———. *The Hour of the Helicopter*. Somerset, England: Linden Hall, 1992.
Bennett, John C. *Social Salvation*. New York: Charles Scribner's Sons, 1935.
Benson, Clarence Irving. *The Eight Points of the Oxford Group*. London: Humphrey Milford, Oxford University Press, 1936.
Blake, Howard C. *Way to Go: Adventures in Search of God's Will*. Burbank, CA: Pooh Stix Press, 1992.
Braden, Charles Samuel. *These Also Believe*. New York: The Macmillan Company, 1951.
Brown, Philip Marshall. *The Venture of Belief*. New York: Fleming H. Revell, 1935.
Buchman, Frank N. D. *Remaking the World*. London: Blandford Press, 1961.
———, and Sherwood Eddy. *Ten Suggestions for Personal Work* (not located).
———. *The Revolutionary Path: Moral Re-Armament in the thinking of Frank Buchman*. London: Grosvenor, 1975.
———. *Where Personal Work Begins*. Extracts and notes from talks given at the Lily Valley Conference near Kuling, China 1-13 August, 1918. London: Grosvenor Books, 1984.
Frank Buchman-80. Compiled by His Friends. London: Blandford Press, 1958.
Cantrill, Hadley. *The Psychology of Social Movements*. New York: John Wiley & Sons, Inc., 1941.
Carey, Walter, Bishop of Bloemfontein. *The Group System and the Catholic Church*. Archives of the Episcopal Church, Austin, Texas, n.d.
Clapp, Charles, Jr. *The Big Bender*. New York: Harper & Row, 1938.
———. *Drinking's Not the Problem*. New York: Thomas Y. Crowell, 1949.
Clark, Walter Houston. *The Oxford Group: Its History and Significance*. New York: Bookman Associates, 1951.
Cook, Sydney and Garth Lean. *The Black and White Book: A Handbook of Revolution*. London: Blandford Press, 1972.
Crossman, R. H. S. *Oxford and the Groups*. Oxford: Basil Blackwell, 1934.
Crothers, Susan. *Susan and God*. New York: Harper & Brothers, 1939.
Day, Sherwood Sunderland. *The Principles of the Group*. Oxford: University Press, n.d.
Dinger, Clair M. *Moral Re-Armament: A Study of Its Technical and Religious Nature in the Light of Catholic Teaching*. Washington, D.C.: The Catholic University of America Press, 1961.
Driberg, Tom. *The Mystery of Moral Re-Armament: A Study of Frank Buchman and His Movement*. New York: Alfred A. Knopf, 1965.
du Maurier, Daphne. *Come Wind, Come Weather*. London: William Heinemann, 1941.
Entwistle, Basil, and John McCook Roots. *Moral Re-Armament: What Is It?* Pace Publications, 1967.
Eister, Allan W. *Drawing Room Conversion*. Durham: Duke University Press, 1950.
Ferguson, Charles W. *The Confusion of Tongues*. Garden City: Doubleday, Doran Company, Inc., 1940.
Foot, Stephen. *Life Began Yesterday*. New York: Harper & Brothers, 1935.
Ford, John C., S.J. *Moral Re-Armament and Alcoholics Anonymous*. NCCA "Blue Book," Vol 10, 1968.

Bibliography 145

Forde, Eleanor Napier. *Guidance: What It Is and How to Get It*. Paper presented by Eleanor Napier Forde at Minnewaska, NY, September, 1927.
———. *The Guidance of God*. London: The Oxford Group, 1927.
Gordon, Anne Wolrige. *Peter Howard, Life and Letters*. London: Hodder & Stoughton, 1969.
Grensted, L. W. *The Person of Christ*. New York: Harper & Brothers, 1933.
Hadden, Richard M. "Christ's Program for World-Reconstruction: Studies in the Sermon on the Mount." *The Calvary Evangel*, 1934-35, pp. 11-14, 44-49, 73-77, 104-07, 133-36.
Hamilton, A. S. Loudon. *MRA: How It All Began*. London: Moral Re-Armament, 1968.
———. *Some Basic Principles of Christian Work*. The Oxford Group, n.d.
———. "Description of the First Century Christian Fellowship." Vol. 2, *The Messenger*, June, 1923.
Harris, Irving. *An Outline of the Life of Christ*. New York: The Oxford Group, 1935.
———. *Out in Front: Forerunners of Christ. A Study of the Lives of Eight Great Men*. New York: The Calvary Evangel, 1942.
———. *The Breeze of the Spirit*. New York: The Seabury Press, 1978.
Harrison, Marjorie. *Saints Run Mad*. London: John Lane, Ltd., 1934.
Henson, Herbert Hensley. *The Oxford Group Movement*. London: Oxford University Press, 1933.
Hicks, Roger. *How Augustine Found Faith: Told in his own words from F. J. Sheed's translation of The Confessions of St. Augustine*. N.p., 1956.
———. *How to Read the Bible*. London: Moral Re-Armament, 1940.
———. *Letters to Parsi*. London: Blandford Press, 1960.
———. *The Endless Adventure*. London: Blandford Press, 1964.
———. *The Lord's Prayer and Modern Man*. London: Blandford Press, 1967.
Hofmeyr, Bremer. *How to Change*. New York: Moral Re-Armament, n.d.
———. *How to Listen*. London: The Oxford Group, 1941.
Holme, Reginald. *A Journalist for God: The memoirs of Reginald Holme*. London: A Bridge Builders Publication, 1995.
Holmes-Walker, Wilfrid. *The New Enlistment*. London: The Oxford Group, circa 1937.
Howard, Peter. *Frank Buchman's Secret*. Garden City: New York: Doubleday & Company, Inc., 1961.
———. *Fighters Ever*. London: William Heinemann, 1941
———. *Innocent Men*. London: William Heinemann, 1941.
———. *Ideas Have Legs*. London: Muller, 1945.
———. *That Man Frank Buchman*. London: Blandford Press, 1946.
———. *The World Rebuilt*. New York. Duell, Sloan & Pearce, 1951.
Hunter, T. Willard, with assistance from M.D.B. *A.A.'s Roots in the Oxford Group*. New York: A.A. Archives, 1988.
———. *Press Release*. Buchman Events/Pennsylvania, October 19, 1991.
———. *"It Started Right There" Behind the Twelve Steps and the Self-help Movement*. Oregon: Grosvenor Books, 1994.
———. *The Spirit of Charles Lindbergh: Another Dimension*. Lanham, MD: Madison Books, 1993.
———. *Uncommon Friends' Uncommon Friend*. A tribute to James Draper Newton, on the occasion of his eighty-fifth birthday. (Pamphlet, March 30, 1990).
———. *World Changing Through Life Changing*. Thesis, Newton Center, Mass: Andover-Newton Theological School, 1977.
Hutchinson, Michael. *A Christian Approach to Other Faiths*. London: Grosvenor Books, 1991.
———. *The Confessions*. (privately published study of St. Augustine's *Confessions*).

Jaeger, Clara. *Philadelphia Rebel: The Education of a Bourgeoise*. Virginia: Grosvenor, 1988.
Jones, Olive M. *Inspired Children*. New York: Harper & Brothers, 1933.
———. *Inspired Youth*. New York: Harper & Brothers, 1938.
Kestne, Eugene. *The Lord of History*. Boston: Daughters of St. Paul, 1980.
Kitchen, V. C. *I Was a Pagan*. New York: Harper & Brothers, 1934.
Koenig, His Eminence Franz Cardinal. *True Dialogue*. Oregon: Grosvenor USA, 1986.
Lean, Garth. *Cast Out Your Nets*. London: Grosvenor, 1990.
———. *Frank Buchman: A Life*. London: Constable, 1985.
———. *Good God, It Works*. London: Blandford Press, 1974.
———. *Joyful Remembrance*. London: Executors of Garth D. Lean, 1994.
———. *On the Tail of a Comet: The Life of Frank Buchman*. Colorado Springs: Helmers & Howard, 1988.
———, and Morris Martin. *New Leadership*. London: William Heinemann, 1936.
Leon, Philip. A Philosopher's Quiet Time. N.p., n.d.
———. *The Philosophy of Courage or the Oxford Group Way*. New York: Oxford University Press, 1939.
"Less Buchmanism." *Time*, November 24, 1941.
Letter 7, The: The South African Adventure. A Miracle Working God Abroad. Oxford: The Groups, A First Century Christian Fellowship, 1930.
Macintosh, Douglas C. *Personal Religion*. New York: Charles Scribner's Sons, 1942.
Macmillan, Ebenezer. *Seeking and Finding*. New York: Harper & Brothers, 1933.
Margetson, The Very Reverend Provost. *The South African Adventure*. The Oxford Group, n.d.
Martin, Morris H. *Always a Little Further: Four Lives of a Luckie Felowe*. AZ: Elm Street Press, 2001.
———. *The Thunder and the Sunshine*. Washington D.C.: MRA, n.d.
———. *Born to Live in the Future*. n.l.: Up With People, 1991.
McAll, Dr. Frances. *So What's the Alternative?* London: Moral Re-Armament, 1974.
Molony, John N. *Moral Re-Armament*. Melbourne: The Australian Catholic Truth Society Record, June 10, 1956.
Mottu, Philippe. *The Story of Caux*. London: Grosvenor, 1970.
Mowat, R. C. *Modern Prophetic Voices: From Kierkegaard to Buchman*. Oxford: New Cherwel Press, 1994.
———. *The Message of Frank Buchman*. London: Blandford Press, n.d.
———. *Report on Moral Re-Armament*. London: Blandford Press, 1955.
———. *Creating the European Community*. London, 1973.
———. *Decline and Renewal: Europe Ancient and Modern*. Oxford: New Cherwel Press, 1991.
Murray, Robert H. *Group Movements Throughout the Ages*. New York: Harper & Brothers, 1935.
Newton, Eleanor Forde. *I Always Wanted Adventure*. London: Grosvenor, 1992.
———. *Echoes From The Heart*. Fort Myers Beach, Florida, 1986.
Newton, James Draper. *Uncommon Friends: Life with Thomas Edison, Henry Ford, Harvey Firestone, Alexis Carrel, & Charles Lindbergh*. New York: Harcourt Brace, 1987.
Phillimore, Miles. *Just for Today*. Privately published pamphlet, 1940.
Prescott, D. M. *A New Day: Daily Readings for Our Time*. New ed. London: Grosvenor Book, 1979.
Raynor, Frank D., and Leslie D. Weatherhead. *The Finger of God*. London: Group Publications, Ltd., 1934.
Reynolds, Amelia S. *New Lives for Old*. New York: Fleming H. Revell, 1929.

Bibliography

Roots, The Right Reverend Herbert, Bishop of Hankow, China. *The Two Options*. The Oxford Group, 1934.
Roots, John McCook. *An Apostle to Youth*. Oxford, The Oxford Group, 1928.
Rose, Cecil. *When Man Listens*. New York: Oxford University Press, 1937.
Rose, Howard J. *The Quiet Time*. New York: Oxford Group at 61 Gramercy Park, North, 1937.
Russell, Arthur J. *For Sinners Only*. London: Hodder & Stoughton, 1932.
─────. *One Thing I Know*. New York: Harper & Brothers, 1933.
Sangster, W. E. *God Does Guide Us*. New York: The Abingdon Press, 1934.
Sherry, Frank H. and Mahlon H. Hellerich. *The Formative Years of Frank N. D. Buchman*. (Reprint of article at Frank Buchman home in Allentown, Pennsylvania).
Spencer, F. A. M. *The Meaning of the Groups*. London: Methuen & Co., Ltd., 1934.
Spoerri, Theophil. *Dynamic out of Silence: Frank Buchman's Relevance Today*. Translated by John Morrison. London: Grosvenor Books, 1976.
Streeter, Burnett Hillman. *The God Who Speaks*. London: Macmillan & Co., Ltd., 1936.
─────. *Reality*. London, 1943.
Suenens, Rt. Rev. Msgr. *The Right View of Moral Re-Armament*. London: Burns and Oates, 1952.
The Bishop of Leicester, Chancellor R. J. Campbell and the Editor of the "Church of England Newspaper." *Stories of our Oxford House Party.*, July 17, 1931.
The Groups in South Africa 1930. South Africa: The Groups, 1930.
The Layman with a Notebook. *What Is the Oxford Group?* London: Oxford University Press, 1933.
Thornhill, Alan. *One Fight More*. London: Frederick Muller, 1943.
─────. *The Significance of the Life of Frank Buchman*. London: Moral Re-Armament, 1952.
─────. *Best of Friends: A Life of Enriching Friendships*. United Kingdom, Marshall Pickering, 1986.
Thornton-Duesbury, Julian P. *Sharing*. The Oxford Group. n.d.
─────. *The Oxford Group: A Brief Account of its Principles and Growth*. London: The Oxford Group, 1947.
─────. *The Open Secret of MRA*. London: Blandford, 1964.
─────. *A Visit to Caux: First-hand experience of Moral Re-Armament in action*. London: The Oxford Group, 1960.
"Calvary's Eviction of Buchman." *Time Magazine*, November 24, 1941.
Twitchell, Kenaston. *Do You Have to Be Selfish*. New York: Moral Re-Armament, n.d.
─────. *How Do You Make Up Your Mind*. New York: Moral Re-Armament, n.d.
─────. *Regeneration in the Ruhr*. Princeton: Princeton University Press, 1981.
─────. *Supposing Your Were Absolutely Honest*. New York: Moral Re-Armament, n.d.
─────. *The Strength of a Nation: Absolute Purity*. New York: Moral Re-Armament, n.d.
Van Dusen, Henry P. "Apostle to the Twentieth Century: Frank N. D. Buchman." *The Atlantic Monthly*, Vol. 154, pp. 1-16 (July 1934).
─────. "The Oxford Group Movement: An Appraisal." *The Atlantic Monthly*. Vol. 154, pp. 230-252 (August 1934).
Viney, Hallen. *How Do I Begin?* The Oxford Group, 61 Gramercy Park, New York, 1937.

Walter, Howard A. *Soul Surgery: Some Thoughts On Incisive Personal Work*. Oxford: The Oxford Group, 1928.
Weatherhead, Leslie D. *Discipleship*. London: Student Christian Movement Press, 1934.
─────. *How Can I Find God?* London: Fleming H. Revell, 1934.
─────. *Psychology and Life*. New York: Abingdon Press, 1935.
West, The Right Rev. George. *The World That Works*. London: Blandford, 1945.

Williamson, Geoffrey. *Inside Buchmanism*. New York: Philosophical Library, Inc., 1955.
Winslow, Jack C. *Church in Action* (no data available to author).
———. *Vital Touch with God: How to Carry on Adequate Devotional Life*. The Evangel, 8 East 40th St., New York, n.d.
———. *When I Awake*. London: Hodder & Stoughton, 1938.
———. *Why I Believe in the Oxford Group*. London: Hodder & Stoughton, 1934.

Books by or about Oxford Group Mentors

Bushnell, Horace. *The New Life*. London: Strahan & Co., 1868.
Chapman, J. Wilbur. *Life and Work of Dwight L. Moody*. Philadelphia, 1900.
Cheney, Mary B. *Life and Letters of Horace Bushnell*. New York: Harper & Brothers, 1890.
Drummond, Henry. *Essays and Addresses*. New York: James Potts & Company, 1904.
———. *Natural Law in the Spiritual World*. Potts Edition.
———. *The Changed Life*. New York: James Potts & Company, 1891.
———. *The Greatest Thing in the World and Other Addresses*. London: Collins, 1953.
———. *The Ideal Life*. London: Hodder & Stoughton, 1897.
———. *The New Evangelism and Other Papers*. London: Hodder & Stoughton, 1899.
Edwards, Robert L. *Of Singular Genius, of Singular Grace: A Biography of Horace Bushnell*. Cleveland: The Pilgrim Press, 1992.
Findlay, James F., Jr. *Dwight L. Moody American Evangelist*. Chicago, University of Chicago Press, 1969.
Fitt, Emma Moody, *Day by Day with D. L. Moody*. Chicago: Moody Press, n.d.
Goodspeed, Edgar J. *The Wonderful Career of Moody and Sankey in Great Britain and America*. New York: Henry S. Goodspeed & Co., 1876.
Guldseth, Mark O. *Streams*. Alaska: Fritz Creek Studios, 1982.
Hopkins, C. Howard. *John R. Mott, a Biography*. Grand Rapids: William B. Erdmans Publishing Company, 1979.
James, William. *The Varieties of Religious Experience*. New York: First Vintage Books/The Library of America, 1990.
Meyer, F. B. *Five Musts*. Chicago: Moody Press, 1927.
———. *The Secret of Guidance*. New York: Fleming H. Revell, 1896.
Moody, Paul D. *My Father: An Intimate Portrait of Dwight Moody*. Boston: Little Brown, 1938.
Moody, William R. *The Life of D. L. Moody*. New York: Fleming H. Revell, 1900.
Mott, John R. *The Evangelization of the World in This Generation*. London, 1901.
———. *Addresses and Papers* (no further data at this time).
———. *Five Decades and a Forward View*. 4th ed. New York: Harper & Brothers, 1939.
Pollock, J. C. *Moody: A Biographical Portrait of the Pacesetter in Modern Mass Evangelism*. New York: Macmillan, 1963.
Smith, George Adam. *The Life of Henry Drummond*. New York: McClure, Phillips & Co., 1901.
Speer, Robert E. *Studies of the Man Christ Jesus*. New York: Fleming H. Revell, 1896.
———. *The Marks of a Man*. New York: Hodder & Stoughton, 1907.
———. *The Principles of Jesus*. New York: Fleming H. Revell Company, 1902.
Stewart, George, Jr. *Life of Henry B. Wright*. New York: Association Press, 1925.
Wright, Henry B. *The Will of God and a Man's Lifework*. New York: The Young Men's Christian Association Press, 1909.

Bibliography

Publications by or about Samuel Moor Shoemaker, Jr.

Shoemaker, Samuel Moor, Jr., "A 'Christian Program.'" In *Groups That Work: The Key to Renewal . . . for Churches, Communities, and Individuals.* Compiled by Walden Howard and the Editors of Faith At Work. Michigan: Zondervan, 1967.
———. "Act As If." *Christian Herald.* October, 1954.
———. "A First Century Christian Fellowship: A Defense of So-called Buchmanism by One of Its Leaders." Reprinted from the *Churchman,* circa 1928.
———. "And So from My Heart I Say . . ." *The A.A. Grapevine.* New York: The A.A. Grapevine, Inc., September, 1948.
———. *. . . And Thy Neighbor.* Waco, Texas: Word Books, 1967.
———. *A Young Man's View of the Ministry.* New York: Association Press, 1923.
———. *Beginning Your Ministry.* New York: Harper & Row Publishers, 1963.
———. *By the Power of God.* New York: Harper & Brothers, 1954.
———. *Calvary Church Yesterday and Today.* New York: Fleming H. Revell, 1936.
———. *Children of the Second Birth.* New York: Fleming H. Revell, 1927.
———. *Christ and This Crisis.* New York: Fleming H. Revell, 1943.
———. *Christ's Words from the Cross.* New York: Fleming H. Revell, 1933.
———. *Confident Faith.* New York: Fleming H. Revell, 1932.
———. *Extraordinary Living for Ordinary Men.* Michigan: Zondervan, 1965.
———. *Faith at Work.* A symposium edited by Samuel Moor Shoemaker. Hawthorne Books, 1958.
———. *Freedom and Faith.* New York: Fleming H. Revell, 1949.
———. *God and America.* New York: Book Stall, 61 Gramercy Park North, New York, n.d.
———. *God's Control.* New York: Fleming H. Revell, 1939.
———. *How to Become a Christian.* New York: Harper & Brothers, 1953.
———. "How to Find God." *The Calvary Evangel.* July, 1957, pp. 1-24.
———. *How to Help People.* Cincinnati: Forward Movement Publications, 1976.
———. *How You Can Find Happiness.* New York: E. P. Dutton & Co., 1947.
———. *How You Can Help Other People.* New York: E. P. Dutton & Co., 1946.
———. *If I Be Lifted Up.* New York: Fleming H. Revell, 1931.
———. *In Memoriam: The Service of Remembrance.* Princeton: The Graduate Council, Princeton University, June 10, 1956.
———. *Living Your Life Today.* New York: Fleming H. Revell, 1947.
———. "Lord, Teach Us to Pray." *Creative Help for Daily Living* (Foundation for Christian Living, Pawling, New York) 28, no. 2 (1977), Part ii.
———. *Morning Radio Talk No. 1, by Reverend Samuel M. Shoemaker,* American Broadcasting Co., 1 page transcript of program for October 4, 1945.
———. *My Life-Work and My Will.* Pamphlet, Christian ministry conference, Concord, N.H., circa 1930.
———. *National Awakening.* New York: Harper & Brothers, 1936.
———. *One Boy's Influence.* New York: Association Press, 1925.
———. *Realizing Religion.* New York: Association Press, 1923.
———. *Religion That Works.* New York: Fleming H. Revell, 1928.
———. *Revive Thy Church.* New York: Harper & Brothers, 1948.
———. *Sam Shoemaker at His Best.* New York: Faith At Work, 1964.
———. *So I Stand by the Door and Other Verses.* Pittsburgh: Calvary Rectory, 1958.
———. *Steps of a Modern Disciple.* Atlanta, GA: Lay Renewal Publications, 1972.
———. *The Breadth and Narrowness of the Gospel.* New York: Fleming H. Revell, 1929.
———. *The Calvary Evangel, monthly articles in.* New York. Calvary Episcopal Church.
———. *The Church Alive.* New York: E. P. Dutton & Co., Inc., 1951.
———. *The Church Can Save the World.* New York: Harper & Brothers, 1938.

———. *The Conversion of the Church.* New York: Fleming H. Revell, 1932.
———. "The Crisis of Self-Surrender." *Guideposts.* November, 1955.
———. *The Experiment of Faith.* New York: Harper & Brothers. 1957.
———. *The Gospel According to You.* New York: Fleming H. Revell, 1934.
———. *The James Houston Eccleston Day-Book: Containing a Short Account of His Life and Readings for Every Day in the Year Chosen from His Sermons.* Compiled by Samuel M. Shoemaker, Jr. New York: Longmans, Green & Co., 1915.
———. "The Spiritual Angle." *The A.A. Grapevine.* New York: The A.A. Grapevine, Inc., October, 1955.
———. "The Way to Find God." *The Calvary Evangel* (August, 1935).
———. *They're on the Way.* New York: E. P. Dutton, 1951.
———. "Creative Relationships." In *Together.* New York: Abingdon Cokesbury Press, 1946.
———. "The Twelve Steps of A.A.: What They Can Mean to the Rest of Us." *The Calvary Evangel.* New York: The Evangel, 1953.
———. "Those Twelve Steps As I Understand Them." *Best of the Grapevine: Volume II.* New York: The A.A. Grapevine, Inc., 1986.
———. "12 Steps to Power." *Faith At Work News.* Reprint. 1983.
———. *Twice-Born Ministers.* New York: Fleming H. Revell, 1929.
———. *Under New Management.* Grand Rapids: Zondervan Publishing House., 1966.
———. *What the Church Has to Learn from Alcoholics Anonymous.* Reprint of 1956 sermon. Available at A.A. Archives, New York.
———. *With the Holy Spirit and with Fire.* New York: Harper & Brothers, 1960.

Cuyler, John Potter, Jr. *Calvary Church in Action.* New York: Fleming H. Revell, 1934.
Day, Sherwood S. "Always Ready: S.M.S. As a Friend." *The Evangel* (New York: Calvary Church, July-August, 1950).
Get Changed; Get Together; Get Going: A History of the Pittsburgh Experiment. Pittsburgh: The Pittsburgh Experiment, n.d.
Harris, Irving. *The Breeze of the Spirit.* New York: The Seabury Press, 1978.
———. "S.M.S.—Man of God for Our Time." *Faith At Work* (January-February, 1964).
"Houseparties Across the Continent." *The Christian Century.* August 23, 1933.
Knippel, Charles Taylor. *Samuel M. Shoemaker's Theological Influence on William G. Wilson's Twelve Step Spiritual Program of Recovery (Alcoholics Anonymous).* Dissertation. St. Louis University, 1987.
"Listening to God Held Daily Need." *New York Times.* December 4, 1939.
Norton-Taylor, Duncan. "Businessmen on Their Knees." *Fortune.* October, 1953.
Olsson, Karl A. "The History of Faith at Work" (five parts). *Faith at Work News.* 1982-1983.
Peale, Norman Vincent. "The Unforgettable Sam Shoemaker." *Faith At Work.* January, 1964.
———. "The Human Touch: The Estimate of a Fellow Clergyman and Personal Friend." *The Evangel* (New York: Calvary Church, July-August, 1950).
Pitt, Louis W. "New Life, New Reality: A Brief Picture of S.M.S.'s Influence in the Diocese of New York." *Faith at Work*, July-August, 1950.
"Pittsburgh Man of the Year." *Pittsburgh Post Gazette.* January 12, 1956.
Sack, David Edward. *Sam Shoemaker and the "Happy Ethical Pagans."* Princeton, New Jersey: paper prepared in the Department of Religion, Princeton University, June, 1993.
"Sam Shoemaker and Faith at Work." Pamphlet on file at Faith At Work, Inc., 150 S. Washington St., Suite 204, Falls Church, VA 22046.
Schwartz, Robert. "Laymen and Clergy to Join Salute to Dr. S. M. Shoemaker." *Pittsburgh Press.* December 10, 1961.

Bibliography 151

Shoemaker, Helen Smith. *I Stand by the Door*. New York: Harper & Row, 1967.
"Sees Great Revival Near." *New York Times*. September 8, 1930.
Sider, Michael J. *Taking the Gospel to the Point: Evangelicals in Pittsburgh and the Origins of the Pittsburgh Leadership Foundation*. Pittsburgh: Pittsburgh Leadership Foundation, n.d.
"Soul Clinic Depicted By Pastor in Book." *New York Times*. August 5, 1927.
"Ten of the Greatest American Preachers." *Newsweek*. March 28, 1955.
The Pittsburgh Experiment's Groups. Pittsburgh: The Pittsburgh Experiment, n.d.
Tools for Christian Living. Pittsburgh: The Pittsburgh Experiment, n.d.
"Urges Church Aid Oxford Group." *New York Times*. January 2, 1933, p. 26.
Wilson, Bill. "I Stand by the Door." *The A.A. Grapevine*. New York: The A.A. Grapevine, Inc., February, 1967.
Woolverton, John F. "Evangelical Protestantism and Alcoholism 1933-1962: Episcopalian Samuel Shoemaker, The Oxford Group and Alcoholics Anonymous." *Historical Magazine of the Protestant Episcopal Church* 52 (March, 1983).

Spiritual Literature-Non-Oxford Group

[Almost all of these books were owned, studied, recommended, and loaned to others by Dr. Bob and his wife, Anne.]

Allen, James. *As a Man Thinketh*. New York: Peter Pauper Press, n.d.
―――. *Heavenly Life*. New York: Grosset & Dunlap, n.d.
Barton, George A. *Jesus of Nazareth*. New York: The Macmillan Company, 1922.
Bode, Carl, ed. *The Portable Emerson*. New ed. New York: Penguin Books, 1981.
Brother Lawrence. *The Practice of the Presence of God*. Pennsylvania: Whitaker House, 1982.
Browne, Lewis. *This Believing World: A Simple Account of the Great Religions of Mankind*. New York: The Macmillan Co., 1935.
Carruthers, Donald W. *How to Find Reality in Your Morning Devotions*. Pennsylvania: State College, n.d.
Chambers, Oswald. *Studies in the Sermon on the Mount*. London: Simpkin, Marshall, Ltd., n.d.
Clark, Francis E. *Christian Endeavor in All Lands*. N.p.: The United Society of Christian Endeavor, 1906.
Clark, Glenn. *Clear Horizons*. Vol 2. Minnesota: Macalester Park Publishing, 1941.
―――. *Fishers of Men*. Boston: Little, Brown, 1928.
―――. *God's Reach*. Minnesota: Macalester Park Publishing, 1951.
―――. *How to Find Health through Prayer*. New York: Harper & Brothers, 1940.
―――. *I Will Lift Up Mine Eyes*. New York: Harper & Brothers, 1937.
―――. *Stepping Heavenward: The Spiritual Journal of Louise Miles Clark*. Minnesota: Macalester Park Publishing, 1940.
―――. *The Lord's Prayer and Other Talks on Prayer from The Camps Farthest Out*. Minnesota: Macalester Publishing Co., 1932.
―――. *The Man Who Talks with Flowers*. Minnesota: Macalester Park Publishing, 1939.
―――. *The Soul's Sincere Desire*. Boston: Little, Brown, 1925.
―――. *Touchdowns for the Lord. The Story of "Dad" A. J. Elliott*. Minnesota: Macalester Park Publishing Co., 1947.
―――. *Two or Three Gathered Together*. New York: Harper & Brothers, 1942.
Daily, Starr. *Recovery*. Minnesota: Macalester Park Publishing, 1948.
Eddy, Mary Baker. *Science and Health with Key to the Scriptures*. Boston: Published by the Trustees under the Will of Mary Baker G. Eddy, 1916.
Fillmore, Charles. *Christian Healing*. Kansas City: Unity School of Christianity, 1936.

———, and Cora Fillmore. *Teach Us To Pray.* Lee's Summit, Missouri: Unity School of Christianity, 1950.
Fosdick, Harry Emerson. *A Great Time to Be Alive.* New York: Harper & Brothers, 1944.
———. *As I See Religion.* New York: Grosset & Dunlap, 1932.
———. *On Being a Real Person.* New York: Harper & Brothers, 1943.
———. *The Man from Nazareth.* New York: Harper & Brothers, 1949.
———. *The Manhood of the Master.* London: Student Christian Association, 1924.
———. *The Meaning of Faith.* New York: The Abingdon Press, 1917.
———. *The Meaning of Prayer.* New York: Association Press, 1915.
———. *The Meaning of Service.* London: Student Christian Movement, 1921.
Fox, Emmet. *Alter Your Life.* New York: Harper & Brothers, 1950.
———. *Find and Use Your Inner Power.* New York: Harper & Brothers, 1937.
———. *Power through Constructive Thinking.* New York: Harper & Brothers, 1932.
———. *Sparks of Truth.* New York: Grosset & Dunlap, 1941.
———. *The Sermon on the Mount.* New York: Harper & Row, 1934.
———. Pamphlets: *Getting Results by Prayer* (1933); *The Great Adventure* (1937); *You Must Be Born Again* (1936).
Glover, T. R. *The Jesus of History.* New York: Association Press, 1930.
Gordon, S. D. *The Quiet Time.* London: Fleming, n.d.
Heard, Gerald. *A Preface to Prayer.* New York: Harper & Brothers, 1944.
Herman, E. *Creative Prayer.* London: James Clarke & Co., circa 1921.
Hickson, James Moore. *Heal the Sick.* London: Methuen & Co., 1925.
James, William. *The Varieties of Religious Experience.* New York: First Vintage Press/The Library of America Edition, 1990.
Jones, E. Stanley. *Abundant Living.* New York: Cokesbury Press, 1942.
———. *Along the Indian Road.* New York: Abingdon Press, 1939.
———. *Christ and Human Suffering.* New York: Abingdon Press, 1930.
———. *Christ at the Round Table.* New York: Abingdon Press, 1928.
———. *The Choice Before Us.* New York: Abingdon Press, 1937.
———. *The Christ of Every Road.* New York: Abingdon Press, 1930.
———. *The Christ of the American Road.* New York: Abingdon-Cokesbury Press, 1944.
———. *The Christ of the Indian Road.* New York: Abingdon Press, 1925.
———. *The Christ of the Mount.* New York: Abingdon Press, 1930.
———. *Victorious Living.* New York: Abingdon Press, 1936.
———. *Way to Power and Poise.* New York: Abingdon Press, 1949.
Jung, Dr. Carl G. *Modern Man in Search of a Soul.* New York: Harcourt Brace Jovanovich, 1933.
Kagawa, Toyohiko. *Love: The Law of Life.* Philadelphia: The John C. Winston Company, 1929.
Kempis, Thomas à. *The Imitation of Christ.* Georgia: Mercer University Press, 1989.
Kenyon, E. W. *In His Presence.* Kenyon's Gospel Publishing Society, Inc., 1999.
———. *Jesus the Healer.* Kenyon's Gospel Publishing Society, 2000.
———. *The Hidden Man.* WA: Kenyon's Gospel Publishing Society, Inc., 1998.
———. *The Wonderful Name of Jesus.* Kenyon's Gospel Publishing Society, 1998.
Laubach, Frank. *Prayer (Mightiest Force in the World).* New York: Fleming H. Revell, 1946.
Laymon, Charles M. *A Primer of Prayer.* Nashville: Tidings, 1949.
Lieb, Frederick G. *Sight Unseen.* New York: Harper & Brothers, 1939.
Ligon, Ernest M. *Psychology of a Christian Personality.* New York: Macmillan, 1935.
Link, Dr. Henry C. *The Rediscovery of Man.* New York: Macmillan, 1939.
Lupton, Dilworth. *Religion Says You Can.* Boston: The Beacon Press, 1938.
Moseley, J. Rufus. *Perfect Everything.* Minnesota: Macalester Publishing Co., 1949.

Bibliography

Parker, William R., and Elaine St. Johns. *Prayer Can Change Your Life*. New ed. New York: Prentice Hall, 1957.
Peale, Norman Vincent. *The Art of Living*. New York: Abingdon-Cokesbury Press, 1937.
Rawson, F. L. *The Nature of True Prayer*. Chicago: The Marlowe Company, n.d.
Sheean, Vincent. *Lead Kindly Light*. New York: Random House, 1949.
Sheen, Fulton J. *Peace of Soul*. New York: McGraw Hill, 1949.
Sheldon, Charles M. *In His Steps*. Nashville, Broadman Press, 1935.
Silkey, Charles Whitney. *Jesus and Our Generation*. Chicago: University of Chicago Press, 1925.
Speer, Robert E.. *Studies of the Man Christ Jesus*. New York: Fleming H. Revell, 1896.
Stalker, James. *The Life of Jesus Christ*. New York: Fleming H. Revell, 1891.
The Confessions of St. Augustine. Translated by E. B. Pusey. A Cardinal Edition. New York: Pocket Books, 1952.
The Fathers of the Church. New York: CIMA Publishing, 1947.
Trine, Ralph Waldo. *In Tune with the Infinite*. New York: Thomas H. Crowell, 1897.
———. *The Man Who Knew*. New York: Bobbs Merrill, 1936.
Troward, Thomas. *The Edinburgh Lectures on Mental Science*. N.p., n.d.
Uspenskii, Peter D. *Tertium Organum*. New York: A.A. Knopf, 1922.
Weatherhead, Leslie D. *Discipleship*. New York: Abingdon Press, 1934.
———. *How Can I Find God?* New York: Fleming H. Revell, 1934.
———. *Psychology and Life*. New York: Abingdon Press, 1935.
Wells, Amos R. *Expert Endeavor: A Text-book of Christian Endeavor Methods and Principles*. Boston: United Society of Christian Endeavor, 1911.
Werber, Eva Bell. *Quiet Talks with the Master*. L.A.: De Vorss & Co., 1942.
Williams, R. Llewelen, *God's Great Plan, a Guide to the Bible*. Hoverhill Destiny Publishers, n.d.
Willitts, Ethel R. *Healing in Jesus Name*. Chicago: Ethel R. Willitts Evangelists, 1931.
Worcester, Elwood, Samuel McComb, and Isador H. Coriat. *Religion and Medicine: The Moral Control of Nervous Disorders*. New York: Moffat, Yard & Company, 1908.

Index

A

A.A.
- a "selfish" program . . . 38
- a "spiritual" program   30, 65, 123
- a million alcoholics in A.A. in America 42
- Akron, Ohio, pamphlet of the 1940's 4
- Alcoholic Foundation . . 7
- basic ideas 21
- basic ideas came from the Bible 91, 97
- basic text . . . 4, 8, 13, 16, 23-25, 29, 35, 50, 52, 68, 91, 135
- beginning of 27
- Bible sources 59
- co-founder Bill W. 2
- co-founder Dr. Bob . 3, 6, 67, 75
- Conference Approved books 44
- "Conference Approved" literature 69
- court rulings that A.A. is a religion 134
- cure 16

earliest 27
earliest days 1
early 2, 6-8, 10, 14, 16, 17, 23, 33, 39, 43-45, 47-50, 52, 53, 59, 60, 62, 77, 78, 83-85, 88, 94, 102, 103, 105, 122, 124
early pioneers 49
early miracle(s) 17
early program 6, 50
early stories 10
early Akron 8
early God-centered program 50
formula for life-change 59
founded on those beliefs 43
founder(s) of . . 10, 47, 69, 86
"founder" Anne Ripley Smith 6, 86
"founder" William James 12, 13
founding 18
founding in 1935 1
"Four Steps" . . . 4, 49, 53
General Service Board . 7
General Service Office 78
golden text of 20

155

has a program 123
"heresies" 14
history and legacy 43
is a religion 73, 134
language 58
make A.A. ... itself your "higher power" (=" "funk hole") 96
medicine 17
moral standards in 84
"Mother of A.A." (Anne Ripley Smith) 86
nobody invented 53
Number 1, Bill W. .. 103
Number 2, Dr. Bob .. 104
Number 3, Bill Dotson 15, 21, 104
"old school" 2, 7, 33
"old school" program .. 2
old-timer(s) .. 16, 27, 33, 67, 119
old-timer Annabelle G. 51
old-timer James Houck, Sr. 53
original program 2
origins of 44
philosophy of self-examination 110
pioneer believers 12
pioneer program 5, 7
pioneer(s) 1, 4, 6, 8, 9, 15, 20, 23, 24, 27, 33, 44, 46, 49, 54, 63, 66, 68, 72, 74, 97, 103, 129, 135
principles 64
program 2, 4, 6-8, 15, 50, 70, 78, 92, 114, 123
program of recovery .. 78

program of yesteryear 123
real and first message . 89
real, early program 7
resemblance to First Century Christianity 5
75% to 93% success rate in early 47
"Six Steps" 49
slogan 44
slogans 49
Smith home where A.A. was born 6
so-called ... miracle .. 30
supposed program of .. 97
Tenth Tradition 70
text 63
the A.A. program 4
the A.A. way 120
the early A.A. way ... 39
the early A.A. program . 2
three first members .. 129
28 Oxford Group ideas that impacted 52
underlying philosophy 91
universalized A.A. of today 45
very first days 52
what A.A. was 47
when A.A. first began . 47
A.A. Haven 20, 28, 30
A.A.'s
actual founding in Akron, Ohio 1
most miserable years ... 2
own comments on the earliest program ... 3
own literature 43
program, "universalizing of" 63
A.A.'s very first group . 1

Index

Abstinence ... 18, 23, 81, 82, 86, 101, 126
Addiction 11, 36, 37, 73, 76, 82, 120, 123, 130
Akron
    a Christian fellowship .. 5
    King School Group 5
Akron A.A. 5, 73
    Bill's involvement 13
    Christian roots and practices 5
Akron alcoholic "club" 5
Akron Number One 63
Akron program
    essence of the 51
Akron's Christian Fellowship 1
Alcoholic 4, 5, 7, 8, 10-12, 16, 18, 24, 28, 30, 31, 46, 51, 54, 81-83, 85-87, 92, 100-102, 111, 112, 114, 115, 120, 127, 129
    That is the miracle of it 24
    willing to go to any lengths 42, 120
Alcoholic Group of Akron .. 4
Alcoholics 1-4, 7, 9, 14-18, 20, 23-25, 35, 37, 38, 42, 46-48, 51, 52, 54, 55, 59, 61, 62, 68, 70, 78, 85, 89, 91, 92, 96, 99, 100, 102, 108, 123, 124, 129, 131, 132, 134, 136
Alcoholism 7, 9, 11, 15-17, 19, 20, 23, 25, 26, 28, 29, 31, 32, 36, 47, 52, 57, 58, 90, 99, 100, 120, 123, 129, 130, 135
Alcoholism and addiction 11, 120, 123
    a cure for alcoholism .. 15
    allergy 30
    counseling 28, 86
    disease concept of alcoholism .. 28, 129
    not cured of alcoholism 26, 129
    nutrition 85, 87, 127
    the Lord has been so wonderful to me .. 14, 15, 104
    with God's power ... 25, 104
Amos, Frank ... 4, 5, 7, 8, 20, 50-53
Amos Report(s) 7, 50
Anne Smith's Journal, 1933-1939 (by Dick B.) 6, 43, 55-57, 84, 96, 97, 135

B

Basic ideas (*see* A.A.; basic ideas)
Basic text (*see* A.A.; basic text)
Behavior Disorder . 28, 30, 32
Bible, the 4-10, 14, 16, 17, 22, 25-27, 29-33, 37, 42-49, 52, 54, 55, 59, 60, 62-66, 68-79, 83, 84, 86, 87, 91-93, 95-100, 102, 103, 105, 108, 111, 113, 114, 122, 123, 126,

127, 130, 131, 134-136
"ought to be the main Source Book of all" (Anne Smith) . 43, 97
Bible, the, as to curing
  Behold, I cast out devils 21
  Jesus cured many of their infirmities 21
  Rise, take up thy bed, and walk 21
  Then he [Jesus] called his twelve 21
Bible, the, as to deliverance
  Who [the Father] hath delivered us from the power of darkness 31
Bible roots 59, 172
Bible study 5-7, 37, 47, 48, 60, 62, 78, 102, 108, 122, 171
Bible's healing promises
  I am the LORD that healeth thee 98
  who healeth all thy diseases 106
Big Book 2, 4-6, 8, 9, 12, 13, 15, 18, 23-27, 30, 35, 36, 39, 40, 43, 48, 50, 52-56, 58, 60, 62, 66-68, 71, 72, 74, 77, 78, 83, 90-93, 95, 100, 113-115, 121-123, 129, 135
Big Book Seminar (by Joe and Charlie) ... 114, 115
Bobgan, Martin and Deidre (*12 Steps to Destruction*) 28, 54

Book of James .. 3, 4, 36, 62, 124
born again . 31, 57, 58, 73, 76, 93, 95, 105, 116
Buchman, Dr. Frank N. D. (founder of the Oxford Group) 31, 58
  Spiritual experience . 23, 77

C

Christian Fellowship . 1, 4, 5, 13, 33, 49, 50, 122
Church participation 5
Clinebell, Howard 28
Conference approved 44
Conference Approved literature 69
  What "Conference-Approved" means 78
Creator (*see* God; Creator)
Cure 1, 9-11, 14-26, 28, 30-33, 43, 44, 47, 48, 55, 64, 65, 81, 86, 88, 90, 91, 100, 101, 103-105, 113-115, 119, 123, 124, 126, 129, 131, 132, 136
Cured 2, 9-11, 14, 16-21, 23, 24, 26, 28, 30, 31, 45-47, 65, 67, 82, 100-102, 104, 111, 114, 119, 127-132, 136
Curing me of this terrible disease 14, 15, 27, 104

D

Declaration of Independence
.... 92
Deliverance 33, 54, 77, 106, 116, 123
Devil, the 10, 32, 70, 76, 100, 124
Disease 8, 14, 15, 20, 22, 25, 27-32, 100, 104, 108, 115, 119, 129, 130
Divine aid 91
"Divine Derrick" 109
Divine help 9, 20, 89, 92
Doctor's Opinion, The (in the Big Book) .. 16, 68, 121
Dotson, Bill (A.A. #3) . 3, 14, 15, 19, 21, 64, 100, 104, 131
Dr. Bob and His Library (by Dick B.) 5, 135
Dunklin Memorial Church
.... 87, 88
Dunn, Jerry (*God Is for the Alcoholic*) .. 28, 100

E

Episcopal Church Archives (Austin, Texas) .. 96
Evans, Rev. Mickey 88

F

Faith that God cures alcoholism
  Christian Healing 31
  Emmet Fox 52
  Glenn Clark 52
  Norman Vincent Peale 17
Family participation 7
Fellowship 1, 2, 4, 5, 8, 13, 31, 33, 37, 40, 43-45, 47, 49, 50, 59, 60, 71, 78, 81, 89, 90, 93, 113, 116, 117, 119, 121-124, 126,
  religious ... 2, 5, 7-9, 13, 14, 19, 41, 43, 50, 63-65, 70, 71, 73, 75, 77, 83, 87, 92, 108, 121, 130, 134
  social .. 7, 29, 38, 83, 84, 86, 113
  with God 23, 47, 60, 65, 70, 76, 86, 102, 113, 123
  with like-minded believers
    .... 33, 113
Fingarette, Herbert (*Heavy Drinking*) ... 28, 130
First Century Christian Fellowship, A . 4, 49
First Century Christianity ... 8
1 Corinthians 13 . 3, 4, 61, 62, 78, 98
"First Things First" 61-64, 66
"Fitz" (John Henry Fitzhugh Mayo) 104
Five C's 41, 51, 52
Ford, Father John, S.J. 44
40 alcoholics ... 1, 15, 24, 53
Four Absolutes ... 48, 49, 51, 52, 56, 78, 84
Four "Absolute" standards . 56
400 times (approx.), God is referred to in the Big Book 40, 43, 91

"Four Steps" 4, 49, 53

G

G., Wally and Annabelle . . 51
Gertrude 91-93
Gethsemane 15
God
    absurd names for 114
    "Alcoholics and God" (Morris Markey article) 17
    Almighty God . 8, 10, 14, 18, 30, 33, 45, 48, 89-91, 96, 113
    belief . . . 7, 8, 30, 33, 43, 44, 47, 58, 65, 67, 73, 93, 96, 115, 122
    commandments . . 30, 31, 33, 62, 74, 78, 92, 93, 98, 99, 126, 136
    Creator 1, 7-9, 11, 13, 14, 17, 20, 23, 27, 30, 31, 43-47, 49, 55, 56, 63, 64, 67, 74, 83, 87, 89, 91, 92, 95-97, 100, 105, 122
    "Do you believe in God?" 91
    Father . 8, 19, 23, 31, 33, 45, 46, 56, 58, 63, 83, 90, 91, 98, 105, 116, 117, 122, 125, 126, 132, 133, 135
    forgiveness 45, 60, 63, 74-77, 91, 102, 106, 116, 122
    God Is for the Alcoholic (Jerry Dunn) . 28, 100
    "Good Orderly Direction" 49
    grace 10, 12, 45, 63, 76, 89, 116, 122, 126
    healing 17, 18, 22, 23, 26, 27, 29-31, 45, 47, 63, 77, 91, 102, 106, 108, 116, 122, 130
    "In God we trust" 92
    love of . 88, 98, 109, 132, 136
    Maker 63, 71
    mercy . . 12, 45, 63, 106, 122, 131
    name of 48
    power of . . 9, 13, 17, 25, 26, 30, 32, 47, 48, 61, 63, 65, 72, 93, 116, 119, 123, 125, 129
    "Radiator" 49
    reliance on . . 8, 9, 30, 47, 56, 60, 74, 102, 113, 122
    Spirit . 10, 13, 25, 31, 42-45, 52, 57, 58, 60, 61, 63, 66, 69, 73, 76, 77, 93, 95, 96, 110, 111, 126, 127, 134
    WHO ARE YOU TO SAY THERE IS NO GOD 104
    Yahweh . . 11, 13, 14, 27, 31, 44-46, 48, 49, 58, 65, 67, 91, 95, 97, 98
Golden text of A.A. (*see* A.A.; golden text of)
Good Book 3-5, 9, 10, 13, 16, 27, 33, 44, 48, 60, 62, 63, 78,

91, 93, 97, 102, 105, 108, 125, 126, 136
What does it say in the 27, 30, 33, 35, 40, 41, 43
"Good Orderly Direction" . 49
Grapevine, the 2, 17

H

"Half-baked prayers" 114
Hazard, Rowland 18, 103
Healing 17, 18, 22, 23, 26, 27, 29-31, 45, 47, 63, 77, 91, 102, 106, 108, 116, 122, 130
Heavenly Father ... 8, 19, 46, 83, 91, 122, 135
Helping others 35
   Faith without works is dead 36
Henrietta Seiberling 169
"Higher power" .. 14, 23, 27, 44, 45, 47, 49, 65, 90, 93, 96, 97, 122, 123
Hospitalization 7
Hottentot 44, 45

I

"In God we trust" 92

J

James, William ... 12, 13, 52, 73, 77
   "founder" of A.A. 12
Jellinek, E. M. (*The Disease Concept of Alcoholism*) 28, 129
Jerusalem Bible ... 46, 48, 97

Jesus Christ . 7, 9, 10, 15, 17, 21, 25, 31-33, 42-48, 52, 56, 58, 60, 61, 63, 65, 66, 69-71, 73, 75, 83, 93-96, 98, 99, 105, 106, 108-110, 113, 116, 117, 122-124, 126, 127, 130-135
God's Son 98
Jung, Carl . 13, 57, 61, 75, 124

K

King School Group 5

L

"Light bulb" .. 27, 89, 90, 91, 132
"Live and let live" (A.A. slogan) 44
Lord 7, 8, 10, 14, 15, 19, 21, 27, 31, 32, 45, 48, 56, 58, 60, 69, 72, 73, 92, 95, 96, 98, 99, 104, 106, 107, 109, 116, 122, 124-126, 130, 131, 134, 135
Lord's Prayer, the 56, 90
Love .. 10, 27, 32, 33, 41, 46, 56, 58, 59, 61, 63, 70, 73, 78, 88, 91, 93, 94, 98, 99, 102, 107, 109, 111, 113, 117, 122, 126, 132, 136

M

Mayflower Hotel in Akron . 51
Mayo, John Henry Fitzhugh ("Fitz") 104

Medical Help 9
Medically incurable alcoholics
. . . . 1, 20, 47, 92
Medicine (*see* A.A.; medicine)
Meditation . . . 16, 51, 54, 60, 76
Miracle(s) . . . 2, 22-24, 30, 31
   mentioned in the Big Book
. . . . 23-25
   "God-centered" . . . of Akron 2
   "Sin-Jesus Christ-Miracle"
. . . . 31
"Mother of A.A." (Anne Smith)
. . . . 86

N

1935 . . . . . . 1-3, 6, 9, 68, 108, 135
1937 . . . . 2, 3, 20
1938 . . . 3, 6, 7, 9, 15, 27, 41, 50, 52, 53, 55, 68, 97
   Big Book written in . . . 52
1939 . . . . 5, 6, 15, 17, 23, 43, 55, 56, 84, 96, 108, 135
93% . . . maintained uninterrupted sobriety
. . . . 48
No significant Oxford Group techniques 50
No Steps 4, 50, 53

O

"Old-fashioned prayer meetings" 50
Old School A.A. 2, 7, 33

a Christian Fellowship
. . . . . . 5, 33, 50, 122
   studied the Bible 122
Overcoming . . 61, 75, 86, 127
Oxford Group . . . 3, 4, 6, 8, 9, 30, 36, 38, 41, 43, 49-55, 58, 59, 62, 75-77, 86, 93, 103, 110, 114, 124, 127
   28 Oxford.Group ideas that impacted A.A. . . . 52
   chatter 51
   life-changing . . 9, 17, 41, 52, 54, 123
   non-existent "Steps" of 53
   non-Oxford Group people
. . . . 52

P

Peele, Stanton (*Diseasing of America*) . . . 11, 130
Pioneer A.A. . . . 9, 90, 93, 97, 135, 168
Pioneers 1, 4, 6, 8, 9, 15, 20, 23, 24, 27, 33, 44, 46, 49, 54, 63, 66, 68, 72, 74, 97, 103, 129, 135
Program
   original, God-based . . . 90

Q

Quiet Time(s) . 5-7, 49, 60, 87

R

"Radiator" 49

Index

Reality 89, 90
Religion . . 13, 17, 25, 43, 47, 48, 54, 55, 57, 58, 67, 73, 77, 83, 95, 100, 103, 110, 114, 122, 123, 127, 134
   A.A. is a 73, 134
Restitution . 51, 52, 54, 59, 84
Rockefeller, John D., Jr. . . . 4, 7
Rotherham's Emphasized Bible 46, 48, 78, 97
Runner's Bible, The . . . 32, 63

S

Santa Claus 65, 91, 92
self-styled Alcoholic Group . 4
Serenity Prayer 90, 97
Sermon on the Mount (Matthew 5-7) 3, 4, 56, 58, 59, 62, 74, 77, 91, 135
75% to 93% success rate . . 47
Shoemaker, Rev. Samuel Moor, Jr. . 6, 13, 18, 49, 50, 52, 54-59, 62, 64, 73, 76, 91, 95, 96, 109, 114, 124, 127
   addressed A.A.'s Convention 114
   Bill W. borrowed from 50
   books (Anne Smith recommended) 6
   personal journals 13
Silkworth, Dr. William D. 9, 15, 16, 52, 53
Sin . . 8, 12, 28-31, 57, 75, 93, 100, 134
   commandments . . 30, 31, 33, 62, 74, 78, 92, 93, 98, 99, 126, 136
   identifying 52
"Six Steps" 4, 49, 53
Smith, Anne Ripley . 2, 6, 43, 49, 54, 59, 84, 86, 96, 97, 136
   journal . . . 6, 86, 96, 124, 127
   "Mother of A.A." 86
Smith, Dr. Robert Holbrook 3-6, 8, 9, 12, 14, 21, 25, 26, 43, 44, 46, 50-52, 54, 58, 61, 67, 78, 82, 83, 91, 97, 100, 108, 124, 126, 127, 130, 135
   Dr. Bob's story 92
   handwritten letter to Bill W. (1938) 50
   sponsee Clarence Snyder 127
   sponsored by 15
   "Your Heavenly Father will never let you down!" 46
Smith, Dr. Robert Holbrook ("Dr. Bob") . . 2, 15, 19, 27, 91, 104, 136
   "Your heavenly Father will never let you down!" . . . 8, 19, 46, 83, 135
Snyder, Clarence (A.A. pioneer) . . . 15, 26, 27, 48, 74
Spiritual
   A.A.'s . . . history 54
   approach 14, 27
   awakening(s) 23, 77
   battle 124
   condition . . . 26, 129, 130
   experience(s) 23, 77

growth ... 5, 59, 64, 123, 135-136
healing ... 26
knowledge ... 59
life ... 123
malady ... 53
not religious, but ... 65
program ... 26, 30, 123
relationship ... 116
retreat(s) ... 127
substance ... 51
The cure is not medical, but ... 16
wholeness ... 43
"Spiritualism" ... 12, 13
Spirituality ... 9, 122, 134
Spiritually ... 87
"Spirtus contra spiritum" . 124
"Step Zero" ... 42
Steps ... 2-4, 8, 16, 28, 40, 44, 47, 49-54, 59-64, 67, 68, 71-76, 78, 87, 96, 114, 121, 123
  "Four Steps" ... 4, 49, 53
  No Steps ... 4, 50, 53
  None .. 4, 38, 46, 53, 61, 69, 71, 76, 130, 135
  "Six Steps" ... 4, 49, 53
Success rate ... 2, 48
Surrender(s) ... 6, 27, 44, 52, 56-59, 67, 73, 122
  at the hospital ... 94
  born again ... 31, 57, 58, 73, 76, 93, 95, 105, 116
  Clarence Snyder . 15, 27, 48, 74, 127
  Four Absolutes .. 48, 49, 51, 52, 56, 78, 84
  help others ... 70, 89, 123
  to God ... 18, 27, 32, 44, 45, 51, 53, 56-58, 60, 65, 72-74, 77, 83, 96, 98, 100, 109, 112, 122, 123, 126, 133, 135, 136
  were a must ... 122

T

"Teamwork" ... 52
Teen Challenge ... 48
Tenth Tradition ... 70
Thacher, Ebby ... 61, 77, 78, 103
Towns Hospital in New York ... 9, 82
Twelve Steps ... 2-4, 8, 44, 47, 52-54, 62-64, 67, 71, 78, 87, 96, 114, 123
Twelve Traditions .. 3, 4, 43, 66, 67, 78, 96, 134
  violates the ... 134
"Twenty Questions" ... 121
28 Oxford Group ideas that impacted A.A. ... 52
"Two-way prayers" ... 52

U

Underlying A.A. philosophy 91
Upper Room, The ... 63, 108, 135

V

Vaillant, George E. (*The Natural History of*

Alcoholism Revisited)
.... 28

W

Williams, T. Henry and Clarace
..... 3, 9, 27, 51, 54
Willpower 90, 124
Witnessing 61, 66

Y

Yahweh (personal name of God) . 11, 13, 14, 27, 31, 44-46, 48, 49, 58, 65, 67, 91, 95, 97, 98
more information about
.... 48
"Your Heavenly Father will never let you down"
.... 83, 135

Dick B.'s Historical Titles on Early A.A.'s Spiritual Roots and Successes

Anne Smith's Journal, 1933-1939 (3rd Edition)
Fwd. by Robert R. Smith, son of Dr. Bob & Anne; co-author, *Children of the Healer.* Dr. Bob's wife, Anne, kept a journal in the 1930's from which she shared with early AAs and their families ideas from the Bible and the Oxford Group. Her ideas substantially influenced A.A.'s program. Paradise Research Publications, 180 pp.; 6 x 9; perfect bound; 1998; $16.95; ISBN 1-885803-24-9.

By the Power of God: A Guide to Early A.A. Groups & Forming Similar Groups Today
Fwd. by Ozzie Lepper, Pres./Managing Dir., The Wilson House, East Dorset, VT. Precise details of early A.A.'s spiritual practices—from the recollections of Grace S., widow of A.A. pioneer, Clarence S. Paradise Research Pub.; 260 pp.; 6 x 9; perfect bound; 2000; $16.95; ISBN 1-885803-30-3.

Dr. Bob and His Library: A Major A.A. Spiritual Source (3rd Edition)
Fwd. by Ernest Kurtz, Ph.D., Author, *Not-God: A History of Alcoholics Anonymous.* A study of the immense spiritual reading of the Bible, Christian literature, and Oxford Group books done and recommended by A.A. co-founder, Dr. Robert H. Smith. Paradise Research Pub., Inc.; 156 pp.; 6 x 9; perfect bound; $15.95; 1998; ISBN 1-885803-25-7.

God and Alcoholism: Our Growing Opportunity in the 21st Century
Dick B.'s 11 years of historical research have jump-started this compelling new theme: Take a specific look at Pioneer A.A.'s God-centered program in Akron. Then, at why they had to rely on the Creator. Then at what A.A. really spawned in the 20th Century, at the "nonsense gods" that have diverted this society from its primary purpose, and at the even greater need for help from God Almighty on the recovery scene today to restore success and assure a return to sound, faith-based, non-profit recovery.
Paradise Research Publications, Inc., 190 pp.; 6 x 9; perfect bound; 2002; $17.95; ISBN 1-885803-34-6.

Good Morning!: Quiet Time, Morning Watch, Meditation, and Early A.A. (2d Ed.)
A practical guide to Quiet Time—considered a "must" in early A.A. Also discusses biblical roots, history, helpful books, and how to. Paradise Research Pub.; 154 pp.; 6 x 9; perfect bound; 1998; $16.95; ISBN: 1-885803-22-2.

Making Known the Biblical History and Roots of Alcoholics Anonymous: An Eleven-Year Research, Writing, Publishing, and Fact Dissemination Project
A detailed bibliography and inventory of more than 23,900 historical books, articles, pamphlets, papers, videos, audio tapes, news clippings, and other archival materials accumulated in the past eleven years and used in the research and publication of Dick B.'s 18 published titles on A.A.'s history and biblical roots.
Paradise Research Publications, Inc.; 153 pp.; 8 1/2 x 11; spiral bound; 2001; $24.95; ISBN: 1-885803-32-X.

New Light on Alcoholism: God, Sam Shoemaker, and A.A. (Second Edition)
Forewords by Nickie Shoemaker Haggart, daughter of Sam Shoemaker; Julia Harris; and Karen Plavan, Ph.D.
A comprehensive history and analysis of the all-but-forgotten specific contributions to A.A. spiritual principles and practices by New York's famous Episcopal preacher, the Rev. Dr. Samuel M. Shoemaker, Jr.—dubbed by Bill W. a "co-founder" of A.A. and credited by Bill as the well-spring of A.A.'s spiritual recovery ideas. Paradise Research Pub.; approx. 672 pp.; 6 x 9; perfect bound; 1999; $24.95; ISBN 1-885803-27-3.

The Akron Genesis of Alcoholics Anonymous (Newton Edition)
Foreword by former U.S. Congressman John F. Seiberling of Akron, Ohio.
The story of A.A.'s birth at Dr. Bob's Home in Akron on June 10, 1935. Tells what early AAs did in their meetings, homes, and hospital visits; what they read; how their ideas developed from the Bible, Oxford Group, and Christian literature. Depicts roles of A.A. founders and their

wives; Henrietta Seiberling; and T. Henry Williams. Paradise Research Publications; 400 pp., 6 x 9; perfect bound; 1998; $17.95; ISBN 1-885803-17-6.

The Books Early AAs Read for Spiritual Growth (7th Edition)
Foreword by former U.S. Congressman John F. Seiberling of Akron, Ohio.
The most exhaustive bibliography (with brief summaries) of all the books known to have been read and recommended for spiritual growth by early AAs in Akron and on the East Coast. Paradise Research Publications; 126 pp.; 6 x 9; perfect bound; 1998; $15.95; ISBN 1-885803-26-5.

The Golden Text of A.A.: God, the Pioneers, and Real Spirituality
This booklet is the second of a series containing the remarks of Dick B. at his annual seminars at The Wilson House. The booklet contains the sincere and surprising credit that Bill Wilson and Bill Dotson (A.A. #3) gave to God for curing them of the disease of alcoholism; Paradise Research Publications; 94pp; 6 x 9; perfect bound; 2000; $14.95; ISBN 1-885803-29-X.

The Good Book and The Big Book: A.A.'s Roots in the Bible (Second Edition)
Fwd. by Robert R. Smith, son of Dr. Bob & Anne; co-author, *Children of the Healer*.
The author shows conclusively that A.A.'s program of recovery came primarily from the Bible. This is a history of A.A.'s biblical roots as they can be seen in A.A.'s Big Book, Twelve Steps, and Fellowship. Paradise Research Publications; 264 pp.; 6 x 9; perfect bound; 1997; $17.95; ISBN 1-885803-16-8.

The Oxford Group & Alcoholics Anonymous (Second Edition)
Foreword by Rev. T. Willard Hunter; author, columnist, Oxford Group activist.
A comprehensive history of the origins, principles, practices, and contributions to A.A. of "A First Century Christian Fellowship" (also known as the Oxford Group) of which A.A. was an integral part in the developmental period between 1931 and 1939. Paradise Research Publications; 432 pp.; 6 x 9; perfect bound; 1998; $17.95; ISBN 1-885803-19-2. (Previous title: *Design for Living*).

That Amazing Grace: The Role of Clarence and Grace S. in Alcoholics Anonymous
Foreword by Harold E. Hughes, former U.S. Senator from, and Governor of, Iowa.
Precise details of early A.A.'s spiritual practices—from the recollections of Grace S., widow of A.A. pioneer, Clarence S. Paradise Research Pub.; 160 pp.; 6 x 9; perfect bound; 1996; $16.95; ISBN 1-885803-06-0.

Turning Point: A History of Early A.A.'s Spiritual Roots and Successes
Fwd. by Paul Wood, Ph.D., Pres., Nat. Council on Alcoholism and Drug Dependence.
Turning Point is a comprehensive history of early A.A.'s spiritual roots and successes. It is the culmination of six years of research, traveling, and interviews. Dick B.'s latest title shows specifically what the Twelve Step pioneers borrowed from: (1) The Bible; (2) The Rev. Sam Shoemaker's teachings; (3) The Oxford Group; (4) Anne Smith's Journal; and (5) meditation periodicals and books, such as *The Upper Room*. Paradise Research Publications; 776 pp.; 6 x 9; perfect bound; 1997; $29.95; ISBN: 1-885803-07-9.

Utilizing Early A.A.'s Spiritual Roots for Recovery Today
This booklet is the first of a series containing the remarks of Dick B. at his annual seminars at The Wilson House—birthplace of A.A. co-founder Bill Wilson. It is intended as a guide for study groups who wish to apply today the highly successful program and principles of early A.A.. Paradise Research Publications; 106 pp.; 6 x 9; perfect bound; 2000; $14.95; ISBN 1-885803-28-1.

Why Early A.A. Succeeded: The Good Book in Alcoholics Anonymous Yesterday and Today
Foreword by Jeffrey H. Boyd, M.D., M. Div., M.P.H.; Chairman of Psychiatry, Waterbury Hospital, Waterbury, CT; Ordained Episcopal Minister; Chairman of the New England Evangelical Theological Society.
Paradise Research Pub.; approx 330 pp.; 6 x 9; perfect bound; 2001; $17.95; ISBN 1-885803-31-1.

Paradise Research Publications, Inc.
P.O. Box 837
Kihei, HI 96753-0837
Phone/fax: 808 874 4876
Email: dickb@dickb.com

URL: http://www.dickb.com/index.shtml

About the Author

Dick B. is an active, recovered member of Alcoholics Anonymous; a retired attorney; and a Bible student. He has sponsored more than eighty men in their recovery from alcoholism. Consistent with A.A.'s traditions of anonymity, he uses the pen name "Dick B."

Dick is the father of two married sons (Ken and Don) and a grandfather. As a young man, he did a stint as a newspaper reporter. He attended the University of California, Berkeley, where he received his A.A. degree in economics with honors, and was elected to Phi Beta Kappa in his Junior year. In the United States Army, he was an Information Education Specialist. He received his A.B. and J.D. degrees from Stanford University, and was Case Editor of the Stanford Law Review. Dick became interested in Bible study in his childhood Sunday School and was much inspired by his mother's almost daily study of Scripture. He joined, and later became president of, a Community Church affiliated with the United Church of Christ. By 1972, he was studying the origins of the Bible and began traveling abroad in pursuit of that subject. In 1979, he became much involved in a Biblical research, teaching, and fellowship ministry. In his community life, he was president of a merchants' council, Chamber of Commerce, church retirement center, and homeowners' association. He served on a public district board and was active in a service club.

In 1986, he was felled by alcoholism, gave up his law practice, and began recovery as a member of the Fellowship of Alcoholics Anonymous. In 1990, his interest in A.A.'s Biblical/Christian roots was sparked by his attendance at A.A.'s International Convention in Seattle. Since then, he has traveled widely; researched at archives, and at public and seminary libraries; interviewed scholars, historians, clergy, A.A. "old timers" and survivors; and participated in conferences, programs, panels, and seminars on early A.A.'s spiritual history.

Dick B.'s body of work on the history and successes of early Alcoholics Anonymous includes seminars, books, articles, radio interviews, videos, audio cassettes tapes, and newspaper articles. They show how the basic, and highly successful, biblical ideas used by early AAs can be valuable tools for success in today's A.A. Also, the religious and recovery communities are using his research and titles to work more effectively with alcoholics, addicts, and others involved in Twelve Step programs.

He has had eighteen titles published about the history and successes of early A.A.: (1) *Anne Smith's Journal, 1933-1939: A.A.'s Principles of Success*; (2) *By the Power of God: A Guide to Early A.A. Groups & Forming Similar Groups Today*; (3) *Courage to Change: The Christian Roots of the Twelve-Step Movement* (with Bill Pittman); (4) *Dr. Bob and His Library: A Major A.A. Spiritual Source*; (5) *God and Alcoholism: Our Growing Opportunity in the 21st Century*; (6) *Good Morning!: Quiet Time, Morning Watch, Meditation, and Early A.A.*; (7) *Hope!: The Story of Geraldine D., Alina Lodge, & Recovery*; (8) *Making Known the Biblical History and Roots of Alcoholics Anonymous: An Eleven-Year Research, Writing, Publishing, and Fact Dissemination Project*; (9) *New Light on Alcoholism: God, Sam Shoemaker, and A.A.*; (10) *The Akron Genesis of Alcoholics Anonymous*; (11) *The Books Early AAs Read for Spiritual Growth*; (12) *The Golden Text of A.A.*; (13) *The Good Book and The Big Book: A.A.'s Roots in the Bible*; (14) *The Oxford Group & Early Alcoholics Anonymous: A Design for Living that Works!*; (15) *That Amazing Grace: The Role of Clarence and Grace S. in Alcoholics Anonymous*; (16) *Turning Point: A History of Early A.A.'s Spiritual Roots and Successes*; (17) *Utilizing Early A.A.''s Spiritual Roots for Recovery Today*; and (18) *Why Early A.A. Succeeded: The Good Book in Alcoholics Anonymous Yesterday and Today (A Bible Study Primer for AAs and other 12-Steppers)*.

These have been discussed in newspaper articles and reviewed in *Library Journal, Bookstore Journal, For A Change, The Living Church, Faith at Work, Sober Times, Episcopal Life, Recovery News, Ohioana Quarterly, The PHOENIX, MRA Newsletter*, and the *Saint Louis University Theology Digest*.

Dick now, and usually, has several works in progress. Much of his research and writing is done in collaboration with his older son, Ken, who holds B.A., B.Th., and M.A. degrees. Ken has been a lecturer in New Testament Greek at a Bible college and a lecturer in Fundamentals of Oral Communication at San Francisco State University. Ken is a computer specialist.

Dick is a member of the American Historical Association, Maui Writers Guild, Christian association for Psychological Studies, and The Authors' Guild. He speaks at conferences, panels, seminars, and interviews.

How to Order Dick B.'s Historical Titles on Early A.A.

Order Form

Qty.

Send: ____ *Anne Smith's Journal, 1933-1939* @ $16.95 ea. $_____

____ *By the Power of God* (early A.A. groups today) @ $16.95 ea. $_____

____ *Cured!* ** @ $17.95 ea. $_____

____ *Dr. Bob and His Library* @ $15.95 ea. $_____

____ *God and Alcoholism* @ $17.95 ea. $_____

____ *Good Morning!* (Quiet Time, etc.) @ $16.95 ea. $_____

____ *Making Known the Biblical History and Roots of Alcoholics Anonymous* ** @ $24.95 ea. $_____

____ *New Light on Alcoholism* (Sam Shoemaker) @ $24.95 ea. $_____

____ *The Akron Genesis of Alcoholics Anonymous* @ $17.95 ea. $_____

____ *The Books Early AAs Read for Spiritual Growth* @ $15.95 ea. $_____

____ *The Golden Text of A.A.* @ $14.95 ea. $_____

____ *The Good Book and The Big Book* (Bible roots) @ $17.95 ea. $_____

____ *The Oxford Group & Alcoholics Anonymous* @ $17.95 ea. $_____

____ *That Amazing Grace* (Clarence and Grace S.) @ $16.95 ea. $_____

____ *Turning Point* (a comprehensive history) @ $29.95 ea. $_____

____ *Utilizing Early A.A.'s Spiritual Roots ... Today* @ $14.95 ea. $_____

____ *Why Early A.A. Succeeded* @ $17.95 ea. $_____

[For 15 vol. Set, put $199.95 in "Subtotal" & $25.00 in S&H] Subtotal $_____
** **Cured!** & **Making Known** not included in 15 vol. Set
Shipping and Handling (within the U.S.)***   Shipping and Handling (S&H) $_____
   Add 10% of retail price (minimum $4.50)
*** **Please contact us for S&H charges for non-U.S. orders** Total Enclosed $_____

Name: _____ (as it appears on your credit card, if using one)

Address: _____ E-mail: _____

City: _____ State: ____ Zip: _____

CC #: _____ MC VISA AMEX DISC Exp. _____

Tel.: _____ Signature _____

Special Value. Get the Set!

If purchased separately, Dick B.'s 15 titles would normally sell for US$274.25, plus Shipping and Handling (S&H). Using this Order Form, you may purchase sets of all 15 titles for **only US$199.95 per set**, plus US$25.00 for S&H (USPS Priority Mail). **Please mail this Order Form,** along with your check or money order—in U.S. dollars drawn on a U.S. bank and made payable to **"Dick B."**—to: Dick B., c/o Good Book Publishing Co., P.O. Box 837, Kihei, HI 96753-0837.